Curious Commercials

And Other Reflections On Christmas

Daniel J. Weitner

CSS Publishing Company, Inc., Lima, Ohio

CURIOUS COMMERCIALS

Library of Congress Cataloging-in-Publication Data

Weitner, Daniel J., 1948-
    Curious commercials : and other reflections on Christmas / Daniel J. Weitner.
        p.   cm.
    ISBN 0-7880-1758-6 (alk. paper)
    1. Christmas sermons. 2. Advent—Meditations. 3. Sermons, American. I. Title.
BV4257 .W45 2000
252'.615—dc21   00-034303
                                                                              CIP

This book is available in the following formats, listed by ISBN:
    0-7880-1758-6   Book
    0-7880-1589-3   Disk
    0-7880-1770-5   Sermon Prep

For more information about CSS Publishing Company resources, visit our website at
www.csspub.com.

PRINTED IN U.S.A.

It was the people I am blessed to call my family who were the driving force behind this project. So to you, Lynne, my dearest love, friend, and wife ... to you, Kyrsten, Shana, and Daniel E., my super growing-up and grown-up children ... to you, Mom Evans ... and to you, Dad Weitner, I dedicate the book.

And thank you, Lord Jesus Christ, wonderful Redeemer! Thank you for being the living Word that inspires each word of praise.

Table Of Contents

Preface

Psalm 119:105

"I'm dreaming of a white Christmas ..."

Okay, I'll confess: This life-long Northeasterner has come to associate Christmas with cold, gray skies and snow, and I've had to remind myself more than once that Jesus' birth was a gift of God which was made totally irrespective of weather or any other natural phenomenon. In fact, the Nativity may well not have taken place in winter at all. Jesus' advent could have happened in the springtime, in a land which rarely saw snow.

Here's the point: As you read this book, make it a habit to have a Bible available. Open it. Read it. Mark it. Why? Because human words and opinions are always superseded by God's Word. Even if I included something which you find personally to be a "dud," God never misses the target. If God wants you to get a message, it will be revealed to you in the Scripture. Pray for understanding.

Introduction

John 3:16

The shore town at the southernmost tip of our little state features not one, but three, Christmas shops which are open year 'round. One of them features boutique-styled (and -priced!) ornaments and gifts. Another has more inexpensive Christmas accouterment, made more of plastic than metal or stone.

In the third shop, which has some unusual holiday items, my eye was caught by a book I'd never seen before, though it was published a few years ago. An artist made the mold for a figurine that portrays a major scene of the story.

I don't recall the name of the little novel, but I do recall its theme: Santa Claus kneeling at the foot of the manger in which the infant Jesus is lying.

Far too often, Santa is the center of Christmas celebration. The problem is that Santa gives without making a single demand on those to whom he dispenses presents. Not so with Jesus. He wants something from you: your devotion; your allegiance. He wants you to trust his word, that he has power to forgive your sins and grant you eternal life.

Jesus Christ promises that, and he can and will deliver on the promise. Santa Claus can't.

Every family that observes Christmas — whether it be a family of one, two, three, or more — has its own story to tell, for each celebrates the day in a different way, and each has had circumstances like no other. The cat that took up residence in the upper branches of the Christmas tree ... the time Uncle Bill and Aunt Mary surprised everyone by singing "Joy To The World" in perfect harmony (nobody ever knew they sang at all) ... the pageant at which your boisterous little boy played the part of Joseph with quiet, dignified reverence ... the year everyone ate the Christmas fruitcake and declared it "delicious."

There is *one* story, however, that ought to be universal to Christmas celebration: "For God so loved the world that he gave his only Son, so that everyone who believes in him may not perish but may have eternal life" (John 3:16).

May your family, whatever its Christmas stories, share that one, singular story, and bow in awe, adoration, love, and faith before the gift of Jesus Christ, who is both Savior and Lord for eternity.

1
Stolen Identities

Hebrews 1:3

Freddie Cochrane was the reigning welterweight boxing champion from 1941 to 1946. No fighter either before or after him has been able to match the record. They say that records are made to be broken, but Freddie's achievement is going to be around for a long time to come.

On the fiftieth anniversary of his retirement from the ring, the man they knew as "Red" in his heyday was interviewed by a journalist from the most prestigious magazine in the sport. Red's life was chronicled from his youthful days as an aspiring boxer to his record-breaking performance at the apex of his strength and agility to his disappearance from mainstream society, his inability to keep either a job or a marriage, his punch-drunk depression, and finally, his lonely days as an old man, rejected and abandoned by an uncaring daughter.

The problem with the story is that not one word of it is true. Not because the article's author played fast and loose with the facts. But because the man who granted the interview was not Red. He was a brash, masterful fraud who managed to pull off a sham that ultimately embroiled everyone at the magazine in a multimillion-dollar lawsuit.

The real Freddie Cochrane had actually died three years before. It turns out he was nothing like the image that had been portrayed by the man posing as the fighter. After retiring from the ring, Red got a job that didn't make him a millionaire, but paid the bills and put food on the table.

He associated with people. He married only once. His mental faculties didn't abandon him until the very end of his life. And not only did his daughter not move away to avoid him, but visited him almost every day.

Stolen identities. All it takes is a bit of intelligence, a glib tongue, a buck to be made, or some power to be grabbed. There are people who would just love to separate you from your name, your reputation, your peace of mind, and anything else you may have earned along the way, provided there is something to be gained by the pilferage.

You see it in the news almost every day.

Somebody gets a uniform and a badge that look a lot like those worn by utility workers. He convinces the homeowner there's a problem with the gas lines in town and has to inspect the premises. By the time the owner realizes what's happened, the guy's gone — along with jewelry, cash, and anything else that can be stuffed into a bag.

Somebody hangs a bunch of realistic-looking diplomas on an office wall, and hangs out a shingle indicating a new doctor's office is open for business in the neighborhood. Problem is, the man's a predator who's never seen the inside of a medical school. Several women are assaulted under anesthesia before the pattern of abuse is noted. By the time authorities arrive, the shingle, the sheepskins, and the phony physician have vanished.

And then there are those who've stolen an identity, but they aren't as easily detected. Because they represent something that's become an accepted part of the culture. It seems innocent enough. Benign. Sweet. But it's subtle. Like a subliminal message. For most of us, it's just there. Something on the order of elevator music: unless you concentrate on it, you don't really know it's playing.

What's the grand larceny? What's been stolen?

Christmas.

What are you saying? That the identity of Christmas is one of the things that's been changed? Without my realizing it? It seems the same now as it always did!

12

Exactly. Just my point. That Christmas appears not to be different is actually proof it's been altered. For so long that everything seems intact, normal, and in place. I can prove it. For just a second, close your eyes and think about a Christmas scene. Now freeze that image.

What do you see? Snow falling on silent streets which are lined with houses ablaze in a thousand lights of red, green, blue, and white? Or Santa Claus laughing, aloft in his crimson sleigh, equipped with an enormous sack which bursts with toys and goodies for the children? Or malls filling with shoppers who actually deign to speak civilly to one another?

What do you see? Soldiers casting aside their weapons and embracing old enemies as brothers and sisters, as universal peace finally envelops the earth and makes all people realize there is no difference at all among themselves?

What do you see? Dickens' classic tale, *A Christmas Carol* or O. Henry's touching story, "The Gift of the Magi" ... or Menotti's evocative opera, *Amahl and the Night Visitors* or Humperdinck's musical fantasy, *Hansel and Gretel*?

What do you see? The pear trees? The seven swans a-swimming? Or the presents? Or the pastries? Or the parties?

Am I right?

They are symbols, these things. Inexact representations, dim reflections, distant cousins of Christmas. But Christmas they are not. But we've been sold on the idea that they are. And that's where the problem lies.

A masterful job at stealing an identity, wouldn't you say? Here's what we've been told: *Santa* is Christmas; *snow* is Christmas; *Frosty* is Christmas; the *tree* is Christmas; the *delight* is Christmas; the *warmth* is Christmas; the *feeling of peace* is Christmas. The problem with these stories is that, like the article about Freddie Cochrane, they aren't true. Not one word. It turns out that Christmas is nothing like the image that has been portrayed.

The author of Hebrews opens the book with a statement that ought to jolt us wide awake around this time of year. Ready? Here it is:

In the past, God spoke to our forebears through the prophets ... but in these last days he has spoken to us by his Son. [This] Son is the radiance of God's glory and the exact representation of his Being, sustaining all things by his powerful word.

Do you see? You can no more declare Christmas equal to flying reindeer and roasting chestnuts than I can claim myself to be President of the United States. Jesus is not almost the representation of God. He is the exact representation. Jesus is not one son of God. He is the only-begotten Son. Jesus does not just closely mirror the nature, person, and mind of God. When you look at Jesus, and hear him speak, you see directly God's nature, person, and mind.

Christmas is not a day to celebrate commercial success. Christmas is not a day to congratulate human goodness. Christmas is the birth of Emmanuel. God-with-us. The Lord Jesus. The Savior.

Anything else is just a stolen identity.

2
Waiting Room

Isaiah 40:31

The first thing you find out when you enter today's typical hospital is about its nursing department: It's understaffed and overworked.

The second thing you discover in a hospital where nurses are attempting to perform a dozen functions at once is the art of waiting. For everything. It's the kind of thing that makes you alternately boil with frustration when the simplest request isn't answered promptly, and coo in sympathy when you see how many have to be served by so few.

We were caught in that cycle of anger and understanding a few years ago, when my mother was a patient in a local medical center. A few minutes spent waiting for a bedpan can seem like hours. Getting a response when asking for medication can seem like days spent in the process. And word on test results from the lab can seem an eternity in coming.

There's a real temptation to stand by and say to yourself, "Well, they're the experts; they know better; if there were a real problem, they'd be here." There's a kind of seduction that happens in situations like that — apathy calling your name and sweetly suggesting that you really ought to sit down in the visitor's chair, wring your hands, mutter and sputter under your breath, condemn the workers, and basically do nothing while waiting for something to happen.

It admittedly takes a little extra push, a bit of "ummph" to act instead of vegetate. But it's worth it. It's worth it to say, "We need help now!" It's worth it to walk to the supply closet and get what everyone's too busy to get. It's worth it to call and get answers to all those nagging little questions you may have.

Particularly if you happen to love the person who's suffering. And especially if you know she'd do the same thing for you in an instant, if the roles were reversed.

Advent is widely regarded as a season which recalls a period of longing and waiting by Israel for the coming of Messiah. But it is altogether too easy for us to misinterpret the command "Wait!" as "Do nothing!" *Waiting* hours should not be thought of as *wasting* hours.

Those of you who prepare food for yourself or your family know what I'm saying. You pop a roast into the oven, knowing it's going to take over two hours to cook. Then what? Do you pull up a chair and simply stop all activity so you can watch it bake for the next 120 minutes or so? Or do you get busy peeling potatoes, washing veggies, boiling water, and setting the table?

Hours of waiting are not hours of wasting.

Pregnant women have to wait an average of forty weeks for that precious baby to develop fully before labor and delivery. But does "wait" mean "stop"? Don't believe it! Life goes on. Normal work has to be accomplished. Houses or apartments have to be rearranged. Rooms have to be prepared. For some, natural childbirth classes have to be attended and their principles practiced. Activity has to be maintained or even intensified, for Mom's sake and for Baby's sake.

Hours of waiting are not hours of wasting.

A lot of people are computer users nowadays. If you don't happen to have a laser printer, you have to wait for each page of material to be printed, line by line. Let me ask you, what do you do in the meantime, either at home or at work? You do something else! You make use of the time. You don't let the opportunity slip away. You make it count for something.

Hours of waiting are not hours of wasting.

Notice something of a common thread running through these illustrations? It's the theme of expectation. The homemaker anticipates his or her meal to be done to perfection. Even though it takes time. The mother-to-be anticipates the birth of her child with joy that she'll be able to nurture a daughter or son. Even though it takes time. The computer user anticipates the work he's published on his PC to be a masterpiece on paper. Even though it takes time. The same thread happens to run through Scripture, too. The theme of expectation or anticipation. In fact, the Hebrew word that is translated "wait" in most of our English Bibles actually means "expect."

I don't know about you, but every time I used to hear the familiar verse, "[T]hose who wait for the Lord shall renew their strength" (Isaiah 40:31), I thought of someone sitting down in a rocking chair, facing the east, and waiting for God to appear in some kind of sky-rending event.

I don't think that way any longer. For what God really says is just the opposite: *Get up and at it! While you're waiting for me, wait on me. The world's needs are very great, and I have commissioned you to bear my gospel, my love, my mercy and compassion, and word of my justice, power, and majesty to all people.* "[T]hose who wait for [expect, anticipate, yearn for] the Lord shall renew their strength." You don't get strong by sitting down or lying around. You get tired, lazy, and apathetic.

That's basically what the problem was with so many who knew — or thought they knew — the prophecy about the Savior's coming. They let their spiritual vision get weak. They let their faith muscles atrophy.

So in the end, even though it was plainly in God's word, they never guessed that God might actually come in anything so common as an ordinary human birth. They couldn't believe God actually meant Bethlehem — poor, dirty, little Bethlehem; he must have meant Jerusalem.

And more significantly, there were too many faithful people who assumed that when the Creator said, "Wait for Messiah's coming," it meant "wait" in the sense of marking time, sitting down, shutting up, and settting aside every other responsibility.

Because they missed the truth that waiting hours are not wasting hours, they missed him when he came.

Once again, there's a kind of seduction that happens in situations like that — situations that call for waiting a very long time, such as happened when the prophets spoke hundreds of years before Jesus' birth. Apathy was there again, gently calling the names of the people and sweetly suggesting that they really ought to sit down in the waiting room, twiddle thumbs, curse God for not moving faster, condemn the prophets, and basically do nothing while waiting for something to happen.

It took a little extra inner "push" to act instead of vegetate. Some did act. Mary. Joseph. Zechariah and Elizabeth. The shepherds. Those "kings from the east." And others of living faith.

But wouldn't you say it was worth it? It was worth it for them to say, "I can't see the end of my journey from where I stand; it's too far around the bend and it's too much into the future. But, trusting God, I'm going to rise up, shake off the cobwebs, and go where he tells me and do what he wants me to do."

It was worth their getting what everyone else was too busy to get. A clear vision of the coming Redeemer of Israel.

So when he came, they were able to recognize him.

What about the church of today? What about us? What about you? Would you know the Christ if he were to walk into our midst this hour? What if all the preconceptions you have of Jesus were wrong? What if he didn't have a beard as you've come to envision? What if he were short and had close-cropped, curly hair and Mediterranean bronze skin? What if he smiled, told fascinating stories and joked with you? What if he wore not a white robe and sandals, but faded jeans and dirty Reeboks?

I am not being irreverent; I am being truthful. The prophet wrote that Messiah did not have anything about his physical features that made him outstanding. All his beauty, all his strength, all his glory and majesty, all his saving graces were spiritual.

And the same thing can be said about his birth. As one songwriter puts it:

> *He was just an ordinary baby;*
> *That's the way he planned it, maybe;*
> *Anything else would have set him apart*
> *From the children he had come to rescue.*

But do your plans call for expecting such a Savior? Or do you, like John who asked Jesus, "Are you the one who is to come, or are we to wait for another?" (Matthew 11:3), overlook the obvious? Does the church really want to handle the gritty little details surrounding his birth:

- That Mary of Nazareth, his mother, was an unwed teenage mother?
- That Jesus was born in a smelly, leaky, foul, dark, and altogether disgusting public stable?
- That the baby Jesus wet and dirtied his swaddling clothes?

Can you handle that? Can you wait for that kind of Redeemer? And if you can, are you also able to wait for him in the sense that while you look for his coming, you don't just sit down in a pew and vegetate, as we're prone to do in hospital waiting rooms?

Look for Christ's advent in you. Look for his advent in others. (No, I'm not even remotely suggesting anything like that which the New Age religions put forth, that you are all God or that you are all Christ. But the Bible makes it clear that unless you are born again in him, you're not alive at all.)

Scripture also makes it clear that unless you look for his coming in the situations, opportunties, circumstances, and people that come your way, you dishonor the Christ and his gospel. Remember: "... just as you did it to one of the least of these ... you did it to me [and] ... just as you did not do it to one of these least of these, you did not do it to me" (Matthew 25:40, 45).

Waiting time is never wasting time.

- Did you see a person hungry in body or in spirit? Did you feed that hungry body or soul in Jesus' name? You waited upon the Lord.
- Did you see a person hurt? Did you pray with that individual and ask God's love and your love to be spread as a blanket over him or her? You waited upon the Lord.
- Did you see a growing child whose only input was the secular philosophy of television rock videos? Did you take the opportunity of just a few minutes a week to give him or her the good news that there's infinitely more to life in Christ? You waited upon the Lord.

19

You get point, I'm sure. The bottom line is that if we, the people of the Lord, aren't in the business of expecting, more than anything else, the advent of Christ in our midst in a thousand different ways, and ministering to him whenever and wherever he comes, we don't have any business to be the church at all.

"They that wait for the Lord shall sit around"? God forbid it! The truth is, "... those who wait for the Lord shall renew their strength."

Rise up! Have done with lesser things!

3
Right Train, But ...

Romans 1:22

When, several years ago, I first began attending an academic-religious institute to fulfill my denomination's continuing education requirement, I had to scrape the rust off my skills in maneuvering between New Jersey and Manhattan. Once aboard the commuter train, I began to feel downright self-confident, and once I had reached the World Trade Center in New York, I was positive I didn't need any help at all in finding the subway to my uptown destination. "This is a piece of cake!" I said to myself while breezing down through the corridors to the subway platform. A train was pulling into the station just as I arrived at the platform, so one-two-three, I was aboard and, for once in my adult life, ahead of schedule!

Well, everything seemed great. Until the train began arriving at stations I didn't recognize. Finally, I decided it was time to swallow my pride and ask the nearest transit cop a question. "Excuse me, officer, doesn't the Number 3 line go up to 116th Street anymore?"

"It still does," he said with a laugh, "*if* you're on the *uptown* Number 3. You know what? You've got the right train — but the wrong direction!"

What did the Apostle Paul say? "Claiming to be wise, they became fools" (Romans 1:22).

I thought I had a handle on the New York City subway system, even after many years of not using it. I thought I didn't need to be dependent on anyone's guidance. I thought I was heading for my intended destination. I acknowledged myself to be wise; but I was proven to be foolish.

I don't suppose any one of you have ever had a similar experience. I'm kidding, of course! Are there any people who can honestly claim that they have never once been so self-confident about something that they have then actually found themselves going the wrong way?

I think not.

Whether it's reading kit instructions, or following math procedures, or comprehending classical literature, or relating to other people — or even riding the Number 3 subway line — all of us have found ourselves going merrily on our way, blithely unaware that we are 180 degrees out of sync! It often takes a good shot of truth therapy to jolt us out of our foolishness or stubbornness and show us the right way — the wise way — to go.

The religious climate that existed in Judea at the time that Jesus was born is a perfect illustration of those who advertised themselves as repositories of all the right answers about what God wanted, while they had not one clue about what God really required. For instance, when questions about the coming of Messiah came up, the temple theologians fed the people what would please, and in this they failed to teach what would challenge them or change them. It was far easier to soothe than to awaken. It was less threatening to their fragile egos to "go with the flow" than "swim against the tide."

So when the masses said, "We want a Savior who will throw our oppressors out of Judea, someone who is going to destroy Rome forever," the leaders in Jerusalem responded, "All right, that is what Messiah will do, if that's what you like. He will come with his armies and his strategic defenses and his tactical weapons, and obliterate the enemy. That will be the redemption of God's people."

If you have ever wondered why the Magi found the Judean leaders in Jerusalem, and not in Bethlehem, this is precisely the reason. They had buried the truth of God's word about the advent of Christ so deeply under such a heap of their own philosophy and opinion that they had forgotten it!

As far as religion being the visible part of faith was concerned, they were on the right train — but they were going in the wrong direction. With their mouths they claimed to serve God, but in their hearts they were ignoring God. They professed themselves wise, but they had become fools. Incredibly, it was the Magi, the kings of the orient — the foreigners! — who had to inform those in Jerusalem where Messiah was going to appear. Remember what the Bible says? "... [C]alling together all the chief priests and scribes of the people, he [Herod] inquired of them where the Messiah was to be born" (Matthew 2:4).

It was then that they finally dusted off those long-neglected prophetic words and found that he was going to be born in Bethlehem of Judea.

Well, what about all this? *Great history lesson, Dan, and some pretty interesting information, but what does it have to do with me?* Good question, if you're asking it. Here is how I hope it speaks to you. Think about your answer to this question: Are you on the right train ... but headed in the wrong direction? And don't guess how anyone else might answer. This is something that is strictly personal. And critically important.

It still comes as a shock to many that Jesus did not come to give his blessing to the religious community but to oppose it for ignoring God's wake-up call and putting the people into a kind of deep spiritual sleep. You see, God doesn't want people of religion; he wants people of faith. You can be up to your neck in religion — going to church, helping the poor, feeding the hungry, giving to missions — but still not right with God.

Being right with God involves your admission that you are headed the wrong way. It involves your confession that you've been in a state of rebellion against God. It involves your declaration of dependence on God to direct you to life. It involves your surrender of self, of pride, and of desire, to God's infinite wisdom. It involves your willingness to allow God's plan for your life — not your purposes — to be dominant.

And, most of all, it involves not your knowledge of, but your faith in, the Christ of Bethlehem, who came both to overturn our nice, comfortable thoughts about ourselves, and to get us back on the train — headed in the right direction.

And that's the truth. Not mine, but his.

4
Serendipity

Job 42:3

I had just come out of a local donut shop, cardboard container of coffee in hand, into the late fall chill. It was windy. It was gray. Clouds had already obscured the setting sun, and the sky overhead threatened snow. Just as I passed under a tree that overhung the sidewalk, something landed on my head.

Now we've been urban dwellers long enough to realize three things: first, there are a lot of pigeons in densely populated areas; second, you never, ever open your mouth when looking up at pigeons flying overhead; and third, if anything falls from the sky, chances are that, whatever it is, you'll have to take a shower to clean it off.

In this case, however, the "something" that fell onto my head didn't come from a bird. It *was* a bird. A parakeet. Blue, speckled with green and yellow. A beautiful little creature.

Now if you know anything about parakeets, you're already aware that this bird had two strikes against it. Parakeets can't tolerate drafts. They also can't stand cold. And it had been exposed to both. For how long, I couldn't tell.

Call me a dupe for sympathizing with just about all the animal hard-luck stories I've ever heard. Call me just one more gullible champion of the underdog (sorry — underbird). But I just couldn't stand the thought of a defenseless bird becoming some fat cat's early supper, or next morning's frozen budgie-on-a-stick. So I decided to launch Operation Grab the 'Keet. Actually, it wasn't too hard. Parakeets love shiny things, and as this one stopped to admire his reflection in a nearby 4 X 4's bumper, I managed to put my hand around his wings.

As it turned out, the bird was a lot less weak than I thought he'd be after managing to duck a stampede of homeward-bound kids and a bunch of New-York-City-bound 18-wheelers. Before I reached home just four blocks away, the little critter had managed to draw blood from my thumb and forefinger, and was putting up such a terrible squawk that I had visions of being surrounded by a SWAT team from the local chapter of ASPCA as I approached the front door.

For the next two weeks, we watched the big daily newspapers and their smaller weekly counterparts for word of some pet owner who had lost a parakeet. But nothing ever showed up, so we decided to adopt our little lost-and-found visitor.

"What should we name him?" I asked Lynne and the children. Right away, my daughter Kyrsten answered, "Serendipity!" It seemed like a logical thing, so the bird who had dropped in from the sky took up official residency at the Weitner household, and whatever his name had been before his entrance into our hearts, from that time forward he was indeed dubbed Serendipity.

He made lots of happy chatter during the years after that cold November day. In fact, we're still amazed that Serendipity survived as long as he did. He died only after sharing many years in our household. He managed to outlive several parakeets that were raised in ideal conditions from the time they were hatched and fostered with tender loving care.

According to our dictionary, the word "serendipity" was coined by author Horace Walpole in his tale *The Three Princes of Serendip*. It means "an aptitude ... for making fortunate discoveries accidentally or unexpectedly." Since it isn't every day that a parakeet which makes a three-point landing on a human's head gets to escape the cold and become part of a nurturing family, and since it isn't every day that a family finds such a charming little friend, I would say it was serendipity for both parties.

Whatever you may think of a person who shepherds sheep nowadays probably bears little resemblance to what people thought about shepherds at the dawning of the New Testament. The modern view of work is that the work itself gives a person dignity. Or, put another way, if you look for work and get work, if you then pursue your work with energy and thoroughness, part of your reward for doing it can be measured in the knowledge that you are making a contribution to the community in which you live. You are effective in changing the world for the better. To whatever degree, great or small, your work becomes part of an inheritance for the generations to come.

One of the biblical proverbs speaks about the difference between working and pretending to work: "In all toil there is profit, but mere talk leads only to poverty" (Proverbs 14:23).

Thus the digger of ditches, the creator of computer software, the architect of skyscrapers, the driver of limousines, the teacher, the homemaker, the commissioner, cowboy, and cook are all equal, if they take responsibility for what they do and have pride in who they are.

But in the days when Jesus was born, shepherds were not exactly well thought of. They were society's outcasts. Misfits. Dirty and smelly because of their work with sheep, they were shunned by "refined" people. Considered ignorant and boorish.

Shepherds were not permitted to go where the "mainstream" people went, or engage in the kinds of activities that even the common man or woman did. About the only circle of friends the shepherd had came from his own comrades in work. In short, there was nothing that was considered dignified or socially redeeming about being a shepherd.

Then, on a night that had been ordained by heaven from an eternity past, all the social conventions — man-made standards that had fixed a king's role to center stage and a sealed a shepherd's lot to the shadows — were at a stroke turned upside-down.

For at one and the same time, we saw something of
- God's righteousness ...
- God's justice ...
- God's indignation ...
- God's grace ...
- even God's humor ...

in calling those he did to witness a monumental act of salvation.

God's righteousness was declared because he wasn't bothered by their abysmally low standing in society:

> *I know that the Lord maintains the cause of the needy, and executes justice for the poor (Psalm 140:12).*

> *Truly, no ransom avails for one's life, there is no price one can give to God for it. For the ransom of life is costly, and can never suffice, that one should live on forever and never see the grave ... Mortals cannot abide in their pomp; they are like the animals that perish. Such is the fate of the foolhardy, the end of those who are pleased with their lot (Psalm 49:7-9, 12-13).*

God's justice was demonstrated in that he would overthrow the leaders who put impossible demands on the common man: "The days are surely coming ... when I will raise up for David a righteous Branch, and he shall reign as king and deal wisely, and shall execute justice and righteousness in the land" (Jeremiah 23:5).

God's indignation was apparent when he chose so-called ignorant men, instead of wise, to be visited by heavenly messengers: "Ah, you who are wise in your own eyes, and shrewd in your own sight!" (Isaiah 5:21).

God's grace was clear in that he lavished a supreme gift upon those who, by all appearances, did not deserve it. The Bible confirms this: "Toward the scorners he is scornful, but to the humble he shows favor" (Proverbs 3:34).

God's humor was manifested there on that night of nights with men fairly tripping over one another's feet with excitement and bursting out with tremendous joy and laughter: " 'Let us ... see this thing that has taken place, which the Lord has made known to us.' So they went with haste ..." (Luke 2:15, 16).

It was neither kings, nor priests, nor politicians, nor theologians, but shepherds who were called to witness the miracle. It was not the high, but the lowly, who were summoned by heaven to view the holiest of God's mighty acts, the birth of his only-begotten Son, Jesus.

Years before that holy night in Bethlehem, it was the privilege of faithful leaders and prophets to receive the news that Messiah would come to redeem sinners. "But God will ransom my soul from the power of Sheol, for he will receive me" (Psalm 49:15).

And elsewhere: "Shall I ransom them from Death? O Death, where are your plagues? O Sheol, where is your destruction?" (Hosea 13:14).

These men of God had seen the Lord at work. They had heard his promises. They had marveled at the way God worked out every one of them. So they had no doubt that God would bring about the advent of Messiah, just as he vowed he would, even if it was to be generations in the future. So from the standpoint of kings and seers such as David, Isaiah, and Micah, the promise was as good as sealed and delivered.

Generations later, there were others who would come to know of the Savior's advent — kings from lands far to the east of Judah. They had another view of the promise, but it was still closely associated with the words of God which were spoken to the prophets. Gentiles both by genetics and heritage, the wise men had read of God's favor and kindness extending beyond the borders of Israel.

So when they saw the guiding star that signaled God's coming among men and women, they were certain it was for them, because God had spoken through his prophet Isaiah about this very moment in history.

> *For darkness shall cover the earth, and thick darkness the peoples; but the Lord will arise upon you, and his glory will appear over you. Nations shall come to your light, and kings to the brightness of your dawn. Lift up your eyes and look around; they all gather together, they come to you; your sons shall come from far away, and your daughters shall be carried on their nurses' arms. Then you shall see and be radiant; your heart shall thrill and rejoice ... the wealth of the nations shall come to you ... all those from Sheba shall come. They shall bring gold and frankincense, and shall proclaim the praise of the Lord (Isaiah 60:2-4, 5, 6).*

So from the wise men's standpoint, it was the fulfillment of that promise spoken to the prophets of old. Of that they were certain. No wonder they were bold when entering the court of Herod!

> *In the time of King Herod, after Jesus was born in Bethlehem of Judea, wise men from the East came to Jerusalem, asking, "Where is the child who has been born king of the Jews? For we observed his star at its rising, and have come to pay him homage." When King Herod heard this, he was frightened, and all Jerusalem with him; and calling together all the chief priests and scribes of the people, he inquired of them where the Messiah was to be born. They told him, "In Bethlehem of Judea ..." Then Herod secretly called for the wise men and learned from them the exact time when the star had appeared. Then he sent them to Bethlehem, saying, "Go and search diligently for the child; and when you have found him, bring me word so that I may also go and pay him homage" (Matthew 2:1-5, 7-8).*

But the shepherds had been viewed for too long by the nation simply as a utility. They served one function only. They had been put on earth to tend sheep, it was argued. They were not welcome in other areas. They served a purpose. Period. And that purpose did not include inquiring into matters of doctrine, theology, and prophecy. So they were denied the opportunities given to most other citizens of the nation. Including the occasion to delve into God's word: the law, the history, the prophecy as these things impacted the people.

Can you imagine their surprise, then, on that sacred night of the Nativity? The sky opened, the angel appeared, and the preliminary statement was made that a very important announcement was about to be given. When God's messenger said that, the shepherds may have looked around to see where the high priests, Pharisees, or doctors of the Law were standing. Because it was clear that no self-respecting angel of the Lord would be addressing them, the shepherds. Not them, the scum of the earth. Not them, the unschooled. Not them, the outsiders.

So when they saw no one there but themselves and the angel, their mouths must have dropped to the ground. Their knees buckled. Their hearts beat like jackhammers.

And their minds and hearts opened like roses to the morning sun.

Because, from the shepherds' viewpoint, God's invitation to them that they see the infant Jesus was astonishing almost beyond belief. Before them — the humble, the common, the despised — nestled in a bed of straw lay the hope of the meek.

- The gift of grace.
- The enfleshed Word.
- The Son of righteousness.
- The Prince of peace.
- God's surprise package to ordinary people. Serendipity.

"I can't believe it!" "Let's see what the Lord has done!" "But what about the sheep?" "Let the sheep fend for themselves for tonight." "Yes, the sheep will be safe for now." "We can't hesitate a moment; we'll go right away!" "Praise Jehovah!" "But why has he favored us, of all people?" "Right! We're just shepherds, not priests. What does the Lord have in mind?" "Don't question it. Just get your feet moving!"

God must have smiled at his choice of those who would be first to hear the news. A theologian would have become too buried in his holy books to see how likely it was that there were really angels. A philosopher would have dismissed the whole affair as illogical. A priest would have gotten lost in the temple, offering up endless sacrifices. And a king? We know what Herod thought of the possibility of a throne usurper.

But the shepherds did what anyone who has ever heard the gospel ought to do. What you have the choice to do. They heard. They took the message to heart. They went. They believed. And they thanked God.

5
Getting the Word Out

Luke 2:17

Another thought about shepherds.

If Fred Taylor had his way, we'd be Wyoming-bound right now. Well, actually, we'd probably have been residents of the state for several years by this time, if the man had his way.

You have to know something about Fred's background to understand why he's so enthusiastic about the Rockies. He moved with his family to the American West about two decades ago. Up until that time, he had been a life-long Easterner, having been born in the south Bronx and spending many of his years on Long Island. In the shadow of the Big Apple. Part of the urban scene. Right in the heart of the biggest metropolitan area in the U.S. The cultural and commercial hub of the nation, according to many standards.

But then he took Horace Greeley's advice, "Go west, young man." He and his family packed up their belongings and headed for the mountains. From the most densely populated area to the least densely populated. From skyscrapers made of steel and glass to those made of rock and snow. From the noise of jackhammers, car horns, and the cursing of wild men to the sight of jackrabbits, elk horns, and the coursing of wild streams.

Does he miss the excitement of New York City? Not on your life. Does he plan to move back so he can be closer to 24-hour-a-day convenience? You have to be kidding.

It was several years ago that Fred and I collaborated on a musical work, a hymn for Easter. I wrote the text; he composed the tune and harmonies.

Since then, we've worked jointly on a number of songs. I've spoken with Fred many times over the phone lines. We have also kept the U.S. Postal Service and AOL busy with our written

33

communiques. And there hasn't been a single instance that Fred has failed to extol the beauty and grandeur of the Wyoming countryside.

Periodically, Fred contacts the chamber of commerce and the bureau of tourism. Not only in the place where he lives, but other towns. Villages. Settlements. Counties. The state itself. He asks them if they would kindly send brochures and maps to some guy named Weitner. *Poor man's stuck on the eastern seaboard*, he says to them. *He's part of the rat race. He's bombarded by the noise. He has to breathe the pollution. The fellow ought to be coaxed to move out here.*

So I get literature. Lots of it. Stacks of it. I have a whole section of my library reserved for it. The way I figure, I'll be busy reading about places like Casper, Cody, Cheyenne, and Chugwater for a long, long time to come.

A package arrived yesterday from Wyoming. From the town of Gillete. It's called the "Gillete Relocation Guide." That publication joins similar relocation packets from about a half dozen other places. No question about it: Fred wants Lynne and me to pack up our furniture and clothing, our children, our dogs and parakeets, and relocate out west. The man eats, drinks, and breathes Wyoming.

- He speaks about the clean air and water.
- He speaks about the virtual absence of pollution.
- He speaks of antelope grazing in the back yard.
- He speaks of mountains capped in snow while lush valley gardens grow.
- He speaks about a land where a person's word is still his bond, and where a contract is still sealed, not in the presence of lawyers, but with a handshake.

I have never been west of Cleveland, Ohio. I have never seen a mountain more than a mile high. I have never lived outside an area where the air is laden with toxins. Yet I can see the towering hills, the wide-open spaces, the big sky and the warm hospitality of the place as clearly as if I were right there. That's the kind of impact the words and the enthusiasm of my friend Fred have had on me.

It makes me think of a scene that unfolded a couple of millennia ago. That's when heaven touched earth with its splendor. That's when angels split the night skies. That's when a guiding star first appeared. That's when the shouts of angels could be heard resounding from hill to hill. That's when, most important of all, God spoke. Not through the written word. Not through the prophetic word. Not through the law. Not through the earthquake, wind, or fire. Not through war. God spoke through the voice of a human being.

Years later, an apostle of the early church would write of the event: "... God sent his Son, born of a woman, born under the law, so that we might receive adoption as children" (Galatians 4:4, 5).

But what about those who weren't around to see the grand show? The heavenly host? The brilliance of a new luminary in the sky? What about the masses who didn't happen to be in the vicinity of Bethlehem that night? What about the millions of rank and file human beings who may well have run to the primitive stable and witnessed the advent of hope, the birth of God's Son? God wasn't about to duplicate the event, so how in the world were others to know about God's gift to humankind?

At the time, most people thought the testimony of a shepherd was the most unlikely source of news. Not that a shepherd would perpetuate a lie. It was just that shepherds were supposed to know their place. And their place was at the bottom of the heap.

People at the bottom just don't talk to people who are at the top or even in the middle of social strata. It's unseemly. It's rude. It's crude. It's offensive. It's not done.

Until the days and weeks following the Nazarene's birth. Something had happened to the shepherds that was so extraordinary, they had no choice but to tell the story. No matter who or what they were in the brutal and unflattering assessment of their culture, they couldn't keep quiet. A simple truth in the mouths of simple men can have the profound effect of striking even the most learned and scholarly dumb with awed silence. Evidently that is exactly what happened; for, as Luke reports, "... all who heard it were amazed at what the shepherds told them" (Luke 2:18).

I don't know if the shepherds ever considered what they were doing as having the potential to stir up controversy. I don't know if an uncertain thought ever crossed their minds. I do know, however, that if they did have second thoughts, they never allowed them to interfere with what amounted to emotional spontaneous combustion.

- They did not establish a committee to study the theological implications of the concept "Son of God."
- They did not consult with their religious leaders as to the probability of their having seen real angels.
- They did not make Mary produce a deposition which would substantiate her claim to be a virgin mother.

They merely recounted the experience as they had seen it and heard it.

I have never been near the Middle East. I have not seen Mount Horeb or the Mount of Olives. I have not heard the sound of prayers rising up to God at Jerusalem's Western Wall. I have not actually walked where Jesus walked. I have never lived where the disciples lived on the shores of Galilee, nor have I seen the spot from which the Master preached the Sermon on the Mount. And I will likely not stand on the spot on the outskirts of Bethlehem where the infant Christ was laid to rest upon his mother Mary's bosom.

Yet there are certain things that come to the senses of mind and heart as if I had lived there, in ancient Judea, all my life ... as if I had walked its highways, streets, and alleys so often that I could give you directions to any house, inn, or synagogue ... as if I had passed the hillside livery so often that I could say in an instant, "There it is."

- I can smell the pungent-sweet smell of hay and cow dung,
- I can hear the thin cry of a newborn,
- I can see the night sky bright with angelic messengers, as much as if I were right there.

That's the kind of impact the words and the enthusiasm of my friends the shepherds had on me.

They led me to make a careful study of Scripture. There, I was led to consider other words. About what happened after Jesus' birth. His ability, when he was just a lad of thirteen, to teach those who were among the most learned theological professors of the day.

His simple but powerful way of teaching people everywhere — through storytelling — the love of God and the kingdom of heaven. His criticism of the self-righteously pious leaders of the religious establishment. His concern for the sick, the poor, the powerless, the sinful. His genuine passion that human souls should not be lost in their unbelief.

I was left to wonder. To ponder. To weigh. To seek more.

All because a group of shepherds, who should have known their place in society, rebelled against the conventions of their time for one brief, wonderful moment in history.

One of the most common challenges to the claims of Christianity is expressed in questions like these:

- "How do you know Jesus lived when the Bible claims he did?"
- "How do you know Jesus was God's one-and-only Son?"
- "How do you know Jesus was born miraculously, of a virgin?"
- "How do you know such a person as Jesus ever existed?"

Valid inquiries, these! As honest questions, they demand truthful and forthright answers.

One way to begin to answer those who demand proofs is to direct their attention to those events surrounding Jesus' birth. To Bethlehem. To the hills surrounding that city. More importantly, to the men "... living in the fields, keeping watch over their flock by night" (Luke 2:8).

When the most unlikely person to testify becomes the star witness, people around them stop what they're doing to listen. When a whole group of such persons begin proclaiming the same thing, news spreads fairly quickly that something important is afoot.

And when people who have been ardent skeptics begin listening to what these improbable witnesses say, the whole world begins to rock with joy.

Right down to the foundation.

6
Curious Commercials

2 Corinthians 4:5

When a big New York City church bought a big block of commercial time from a big radio station recently, I had big hopes for great things. And I was wrong.

You may know the Big Apple as host to a wide array of churches, temples, and mosques representing an incredible diversity of religious beliefs. Christian. Jewish. Christian Scientist. Islamic. Buddhist. Hindu. Shinto. Scientological. You name it; it's there.

Generally, radio stations aren't selective about the products or services that sponsors advertise, or how they advertise. If sponsors have the money, station business managers provide the air time.

Some faith groups have a lot of money to spend, and some of these use it in radio ads. As a result, you get to hear many interesting theologies and doctrines.

- Treatises which run from the trite to the thought-provoking.
- Thirty- or sixty-second encapsulations of religious dogma.
- Intriguing little windows which open ever so briefly into the heart and soul of what people believe, or in whom they place their trust.

Almost every profession of faith has been heard from, at least in this part of the United States. Far Eastern mysticism. New Age humanism. Transcendentalism. Zen Buddhism. So I think you can imagine my delight when, one day in early December, the minister of a well-known Christian church took to the airwaves in one of those minute-long commercial breaks.

Finally, I said to myself, *a word from one of **Christ's** folks!* I was getting more excited by the second. *I wonder if it will be a message appropos the season? God's incarnation in Jesus of*

39

Nazareth? The birth of hope at Bethlehem? The angels' joy at see-
ing humanity's salvation drawing near to the earth? The Lord's
decisive strike against the devil? Divine love and goodness con-
quering over sinful hate and evil? Light chasing away the dark-
ness from the souls of men and women, and illuminating the gloomy
city?

I should have known better. "A Confucian master used to say
..." the pastor began.

I was dumbfounded. *A Confucian master? What's he got to do*
with Christmas? But, ever the optimist, my mood remained up-
beat. *Ah-hah!* I thought. *I know what this guy is doing. What a*
clever idea! He's biding his time. He's going to contrast the philo-
sophical ideas of Confucianism with the salvation story of Jesus.
So I continued to tune in.

But I was wrong. " ... So the only way we can improve the
state of the city — and the whole planet, for that matter —" he
concluded with solemn voice, "— is to improve the quality of our
thoughts toward one another. In the end, *that* is our salvation."

That crashing sound I heard in my mind? It was opportunity
falling to the floor, dead. A perfect occasion for speaking the gospel was available. And missed. Hundreds of thousands of people
had been listening, wondering what the preacher would say. Some
of them straining to hear a word of supernatural hope breaking into
the sorry state of human affairs.

But no word of that kind was spoken. No message of Christmas. No disclosure of God's salvation story.

It is one example of what I call "curious commercials."

Curious commercials. *Commercials* in that followers of the
Nazarene are, in the words of the apostle, supposed to be "recom-
menders" of Jesus Christ. Something on the order of living bill-
boards. Paul writes:

> *[W]e do not proclaim ourselves; we proclaim Jesus*
> *Christ as Lord and ourselves as your slaves for Jesus'*
> *sake ... the God who said, "Let light shine out of dark-*
> *ness" ... has shone in our hearts to give the light of the*
> *knowledge of the glory of God in the face of Jesus Christ.*

But we have this treasure in clay jars, so that it may be made clear that this extraordinary power belongs to God and does not come from us" (2 Corinthians 4:5-7).

"Jesus Christ as Lord ... the glory of God in the face of Jesus Christ ... this treasure ... this extraordinary power."

Wow, what an advertisement! Madison Avenue would be proud. Shine your beacon-light over Bethlehem, star of wonder. Hover near, you angels glowing in the night. Shepherds, come closer with your shouts of praise. People, come see what God has done for you!

Curious commercials. *Curious* in that ads are supposed to identify a specific product, but you'd never know it by listening to some Christians.

The Coca Cola Company is not exactly ashamed to say that it makes Coke, and won't you please buy some? General Motors is proud to say they manufacture Chevys and Caddys and a whole bunch of other makes and models and, by the way, won't you please purchase one on your way home today?

But I wonder: Why are some Christians — and especially some Christian leaders — so reluctant to identify the One whose birth, life, crucifixion, resurrection, and ascension are — much more than symbols — the *touchstone* of faith in Jesus?

That's the way it seems to be with the celebration of Jesus' birth — and life — as we approach the end of the century. It's a pleasant "warm fuzzy" of a tale, meant to warm us and cheer us on cold winter nights. The message has become an all-embracing, innocuous, vacuous platitude suggesting that if everyone were just to think good and positive thoughts about one another, and please, get together and smile, all the world's ills would disappear.

You've heard it, I'm sure. *"Everyone's* going to be saved, whatever you believe. Whether it's through Jesus Christ or someone else or something else. What's the difference? God will honor anyone who has faith, no matter what form that faith takes." It's a kind of carryover from a generation ago: "I'm doin' my own thing." You know what I mean, don't you?

Wave the magic wand. Get the ideal mantra. Say the right incantation.

But you know (don't you?): It doesn't work that way. Are the streets of your town any safer than they were a generation ago, because of positive thoughts? Are you nearer perfection now compared with last year, because you believe in your own basic goodness? Are your children free from danger? Have drug dealers ceased dealing drugs and molesters stopped preying on the young, because they have found their karma?

Not exactly.

In fact, the landscape of human history is littered with the corpses of high ideals and good intentions. Philosophies and psychologies have been devised throughout many centuries in the hope of creating order, a sense of balance and peace with self, with neighbor, and with the world. Then, of late, we've been told *ad nauseam* that friendship with Earth's ecology, or with the planet itself, will promote harmony among all people.

Have you seen it? Have you experienced it? Do you note that selfishness, greed, and avarice have disappeared? Do you think deceit, falsehood, and corruption are no longer around? Do you find that hate, theft, rape, and murder have ended? Anyone who tells you he or she actually believes these things is either terribly unobservant, living in a fantasy world, or completely dishonest.

Scripture makes this assessment of humanity's so-called "innate goodness": "The heart is devious above all else; it is perverse — who can understand it?" (Jeremiah 17:9). In other words, it's absolutely incredible the lengths to which people will go to try to fool themselves ... others ... and God ... into thinking that they are all right and getting even better.

Ever wondered why? Ever pondered the fact that we have a habit of creating an artificial aura of goodness around ourselves? Ever considered that we try to pawn off our mistakes, faults, and evils on others, to make ourselves look better?

- *I haven't done anything wrong, officer!*
- *Whaddya mean, I shouldn't have taken that without paying?*
- *It's my right, you know.*
- *I'll sue!*

Do you have an explanation as to why you feel it necessary to defend your words and actions, even when they're wrong? What's the motivation? It is because you and I want to be in control. Captains. State department heads. Princes and princesses. Engineers of our own destiny.

But there are times when captains have to turn to admirals for the best strategy. Times when cabinet chiefs must enlist aid from presidents. Times when royal highnesses are obliged to seek answers from royal majesties. Times when engineers must go to the texts instead of to their own imagination.

And times when flawed human beings must approach a perfect God for their soul's redemption.

In fact, the greatest miracle of Christmas goes a step beyond what I've just said. Because the truth is that sinners did *not* approach God. They did *not* appeal to heaven, even when they were in trouble ... in danger of dying ... and in sight of hell. The Almighty was under no obligation to do anything. After all, he had done far more than anyone would expect he'd do for those who had transgressed his law. God had given them every opportunity to repent. God had given them his Word ... his prophets ... his leaders ... and his preachers. God had given them time, through his seemingly inexhaustible patience. And still they would not come to him.

So God said, "All right, then. Since they won't come to me, I'll go to them." And that was Christmas.

Toss away the holly and the ivy, balsam and snow, Santa and Rudolph, and you'd still have Christmas.

Rid the world of merry thoughts, seasonal cheer, and winter songs, and you'd still have Christmas.

Put presents, tinsel, and colored lights into the dumpster, and you'd still have Christmas.

The truth is that love and joy, peace and friendship, salvation, and life everlasting, are all quite impossible aside from a supernatural intervention. Just ask anyone who's ever tried to find those things in positive thinking, crystal charms, or psychic channeling. At the end of your search for hope along a long, dark corridor among earthly things that will pass into dust, you will see a faint glow, if you are not now near it. That light will grow more brilliant the closer you get near its source.

A treasure ... the all-surpassing power ... Jesus the Lord.

The glory of God in the face of a child.

7
The Dismals

Psalm 45:15

Teachers and preachers, take heart! Not everything you say goes in one ear and out the other.

I've never forgotten a point that was made in a sermon that was given over 25 years ago. Bob Veon was pastor at a church in the little college town where I did my undergraduate studies. He was talking about the joyless attitude of a lot of Christians. He said he had recently read the musings of a cynic who wrote what was probably the most accurate assessment of the churchgoing masses: "It's noon on Sunday, and the churches of America are opening their doors and pouring forth their dead."

Joy and Christmas. They go together.

Or do they?

One day a couple of years ago, I prepared the various prayers and selected the several hymns that were to go into the next Sunday bulletin. I gave the draft to my secretary, who started typing the final form. However, after a couple of minutes, she began howling with laughter. Puzzled, I asked what had struck her so funny. Through tears and giggles, she finally managed to say, "It's in your order of worship. At the end, instead of writing 'The Dismissals,' you put down 'The Dismals'!"

It was a typographical error, but it illustrates something that I have been stressing from the pulpit for years. The Christian's worship of God is supposed to be noteworthy for its enthusiasm and joy. By the time a typical service is over, the people have sung God's praises, listened to and read God's Word, and asked God's blessing for what they will do in his name during the rest of the week. They have been in the very presence of God!

45

However, the demeanor of many Christians upon their leaving the service seems to contradict completely a sense of spiritual exultation and victory. Their mood is one of gloom and depression. They are grim and glum. They are joyless. "Dismal" is an apt description of what they look like!

Are you a "dismal" Christian? If so, let the words of the angel to the terrified Bethlehem shepherds resuscitate what may be for you a much-neglected but important part of your life in Christ: *joy.*

"Do not be afraid," he commanded them, "for see — I am bringing you good news of great joy for all the people: to you is born this day in the city of David a Savior, who is the Messiah, the Lord" (Luke 2:10-11).

Note what the shepherds did. They did *not* say, "Woe is us!" They did *not* screw their faces into looks of despondency and dejection. They did *not* present a dismal face to the world.

Instead, they fairly tripped over one another in their "urgent haste" to do what the angel said to do: Share the glad tidings with everyone. And all who listened marveled at what the shepherds said, finding everything just as they had said.

Beginning right now, during this Advent season, resolve that if you are now a "dismal" Christian, you will no longer be so! More importantly, pray to the Lord that his Holy Spirit may infuse you with such holy joy that you will henceforth be unable to contain it. "*Joy* to the world! The Lord is come!"

8
The Light

John 3:19

Ocean City, New Jersey, located on the famed Cape May peninsula of the state, has the reputation as being one of the only alcohol-free — "dry" — towns on the northeast coast. And although it has gained some of the boardwalk attractions that are so characteristic of the Jersey shore, Ocean City remains a beacon for Christians who come from all over the region for the sacred concerts, church conferences, and evangelistic meetings held at its large enclosed pier.

Just as it is true now, more than a century before the town was re-named from Peck's Island and gained its unique identity as a religious haven, merchant ships sailed past the fine light-gray sands of South Jersey. In the early days, the typical cargo below decks was rum and sugar. Some ships bore fine linen and lace. Others were laden with fruit from faraway ports. A few brought rare furniture.

Winter storms in the Atlantic Ocean are as feared as the hurricanes that can churn its waters any time from late June through October. Knowing the ferocity of wind and wave generated in these blasts, many captains had their ships "hug" the shoreline from December to March, so they would have a better chance of steering, in an emergency, for the relative safety of a protected inlet or river.

The practice of navigating in more shallow water in winter weather eventually extended into the spring, even when storms were not as ferocious as during the cold months or the hurricane season. This habit was always risky business, however. More than a few ships ran aground and broke up in the heavy surf. Others would strike the remains of another wreck and suffer the same fate.

And sometimes a ship would be "helped" straight to disaster. "Mooncussers" and "wreckers" were the looters and thieves of the eighteenth-century New Jersey shore. On a stormy, moonless night, they would tie a lantern to a horse or mule and walk the animal along the sandy beach. Some captain or navigator at sea would interpret the moving light as another vessel, sailing closer to land, and maneuver the ship so as to follow it — with disastrous results. In the confusion of sailors and officers attempting to save the cargo and themselves from the listing, sinking vessel, the scoundrel "mooncussers" and "wreckers" would move in and carry off whatever they wished, and be gone long before the authorities could arrive at the scene.

How unlike the cloudy, moonless, dim-lanterned light that the Peck's Island thieves used, as they moved unseen among the shadows, is the light of Jesus Christ. Hundreds of years before his birth, a prophet said: "The people who walked in darkness have seen a great light; those who lived in a land of deep darkness — on them a light has shined" (Isaiah 9:2).

It is no mistake that Isaiah uses the word "great" when referring to the light that Messiah — the Savior — would bring.

- His was not to be a meager light.
- His was not to be a "dim and flaring lamp" by which to read God's righteous sentence.
- His was not to be an artificial light.
- His was not to be an illumination, a reflection of something or someone greater than itself.

As John the apostle would later say: "The true light, which enlightens everyone, was coming into the world" (John 1:9).

For so-called "enlightened" people living in an age of enlightenment, we sure do a lot of stumbling around in the dark. True, we have put a premium on education. A high school diploma isn't enough any more to land a well-paying job. In many cases, a bachelor's degree alone isn't enough. We have enhanced our educational standards. As a nation, our literacy rate is getting better.

More of us are reading philosophical works than a generation ago. More of us are writing books that deal with the nature of existence.

So to our way of thinking, we've turned on the light. It appears, from our viewpoint, that we're seeing things quite clearly. We say we've never understood things quite like this before. We claim to have clarity of vision.

But in actuality, how we perceive the world without the true Light is roughly equivalent to trying to read with dark sunglasses at midnight in a room lit by a candle. It's as if we have taken Jesus' words — "No one after lighting a lamp puts it under the bushel basket, but on the lampstand ..." (Matthew 5:15) — and turned them on their head. Because in spite of what we say about our quest for truth, there are a lot of us who want to be fooled. Yes, we are glad Jesus the Light has come. Because we love the joy and the peace of Christmas. We love the "warm fuzzies" of Christmas: carols queued up on the CD player, poinsettias at the windows, chestnuts roasting on an open fire, and snow in the air.

We love the story of Jesus' birth as an innocent Babe, too. Adoring shepherds. Lowing cattle. A bright, guiding star. The lowly manger.

Problem is, we want Jesus to stay little. Cute and cuddly. Manageable. Innocuous. Non-threatening. Maybe we want the grown-up Jesus, if he conforms to our dictates. We want him to tell us about the kingdom of heaven. We want him to tell us about victory over death. We want him to tell us parables and stories that inspire and uplift. However,

- We do not want Jesus to tell us about the consequences of sin.
- We do not want him to tell us that Bethlehem's manger is so close to Jerusalem, you can almost see Golgotha from there.
- We do not want him to insist that we give up this or that precious, comfortable sin.
- We do not want Jesus to tell us that if we won't cling to his cross for dear life, then the gates of hell — not heaven — will shut upon our spirits for all eternity.

And if the "sweet little holy child" of Christmas will not remain fragile and dear, we will go elsewhere, to someone who's still warm and fuzzy. We want our itching ears tickled by *soothe-sayers.* We want someone who won't give us hard sayings and challenges as Jesus does. We want someone who isn't so tough. We want our fortunes told by stargazers — provided that stars tell us of fame, fortune, and long life.

We want to be led again into the shadows.

The modern equivalent of a mooncusser or wrecker doesn't lead a mule carrying a lantern up the beach to entice unsuspecting ships to ground themselves. His business is to get you to follow the spotlight which he focuses on himself. The light's dazzling. Brilliant. Colorful. You express interest.

Then he throws you his best pitch. He claims you'll be rich! If you follow him, of course. You'll be healthy. You'll be wise. You'll have pleasure. You'll be transported to a higher level of mind. You'll attain your karma, your God-consciousness, your self-transcendence.

Just follow the moving light, please!

This day, one set of rules. Tomorrow, another set of regulations. A theology here. A theology there. Zigging and zagging from doctrine to doctrine. Shifting like the sand along which the light is dragged from one place to another. Winning smiles and glowing promises. False faces with which to hide from the truth which the naked light reveals.

> *... such boasters are false apostles, deceitful workers, disguising themselves as apostles of Christ. And no wonder! Even Satan disguises himself as an angel of light. So it is not strange if his ministers also disguise themselves as ministers of righteousness. Their end will match their deeds (2 Corinthians 11:13-15).*

Do you doubt evil can masquerade as good? Do you doubt that darkness can present itself as light?

Ask the families of those who once followed someone who turned out to be an imposter.

He was a clever man. His excellent salesmanship was taken by many for sound preaching. He gave gave many people the impression that he was an evangelist for Jesus Christ. He quoted

Scripture. He used biblical terms. He sang gospel songs. He had a pastoral style of leadership.

But what he taught his followers was not the Christian gospel. What Jones told the already poor, oppressed, disenfranchised, and disadvantaged was that if they followed him, gave him their time, their money, and their total allegiance (and, some said, their souls), then he would be their protector. He said he would fight the corrupt, satanic government system that was fighting against them. He said he would work to overthrow their oppressors.

And if necessary, he said, he would take them all to a land where no evil would ever be able to touch them again.

What he failed to tell his followers is that he was a greedy man. He wanted the accolades. He wanted the power. He wanted glory. Unlike the apostle who would not boast except in Christ Jesus, this deceiver wanted everyone to boast about his own accomplishments. He was not following the Christ, but was holding himself up before them as a savior, a redeemer. Not a savior in the sense that Jesus was the Savior, coming to save sinners from the condemnation of their eternal souls. Jones capitalized on poor people's anger over their poverty. He manipulated the gospel to make it seem as if redemption meant having political might. He offered them nothing more than, at best, temporary relief from their feelings of hopelessness.

But when every last one of his hundreds of followers — men, women, and children — were ordered by shotgun-toting cult officials to drink Kool-Aid laced with cyanide, Jim Jones showed himself for what he really was: a mooncusser, a wrecker who led the already-hurt and the gullible to their doom.

In contrast, Messiah's coming was to usher in the radiance of day. It would put darkness to flight. Where the old covenant was "the gospel concealed," the new covenant was "the gospel revealed."

That light would penetrate the shadows. It would reveal sin for what it was: a deep wound, festering in the dark, that grew into a gangrenous evil which threatened to poison the heart and soul of God's creation. It would be the cauterizing and healing laser light.

And from the anticipated pain of this procedure we would begin to turn and flee in fear.

But the assuring voice of the Physician would arrest us. He would say, "It's got to be done. If you would be a person of the light ... if you would step out of the shadows ... if you would be whole ... if you would be rid of your fear about today and your anxiety about tomorrow, then it's got to be done."

I'm glad Scripture talks about the coming of Jesus as the Light. I'm glad it contrasts the *l*ight and the *L*ight.

> [John] came as a witness to testify to the light, so that all might believe through him. He himself was not the light, but he came to testify to the light. The true light, which enlightens everyone, was coming into the world (John 1:7-9).

Personally, I am glad the gospel makes the differentiation, because I know myself too well. I'd go chasing after shooting stars, the sort of thing you find in the heavens above and on the earth beneath — false prophets, astrological guides, superstars and megastars of sports and screen, deceitful preachers, and yes, even the star of Bethlehem — unless I had Someone to tell me that they are only lesser lights, or mooncusser lights, not the true Light.

I am thankful that the Babe grew up to be the Man. I am thankful, too, that he was the Light.

- The Light showed the old wounds of sin.
- The Light revealed the secret intent of every heart.
- The Light interrupted hell's well-orchestrated plan.
- The Light penetrated even to the deeply-hidden corruption of dead religion.

The darkness fought back, in a vain attempt to drag the covers over itself once again. It tried to trap the Light in contradictions, but could not. It tried to prove the Light was not all he said he was, but could not. It tried to catch the Light in even a single false statement, but could not.

And even when the darkness tried to snuff out the flame of the light by taking its breath away on the cross, even when the darkness tried to bury the light, even when the darkness tried to seal the light in an airless tomb where it would bother its hellish plans no more, it could not.

Try as the darkness would to extinguish it, the Light never lost its fire: "[I]n him was life, and the life was the light of all people. The light shines in the darkness, and the darkness did not overcome it" (John 1:4-5).

9
A Matter Of Inches

Acts 26:1

This is a story about Christmas — and baseball.

Right about now you may be thinking that the only possible common ground between the national pastime and the Incarnation is the fact that on the calendar, Christmas day happens to lie midway between the last game of the World Series and the opening of pre-season club meetings. But if you are curious about the connection, you might want to read on.

The 1994 major league season will long be remembered by many baseball lovers as the year owners and players nearly killed the game. Although it was in April that the big-leaguers hinted it was coming, it came as a shock to most fans when a strike actually began the second week of August.

Many wondered why they did it. Far and wide, it was known as a banner year, for several reasons:

After several seasons of steady decline, attendance figures had made a turnaround, and were up significantly around the country.

A number of records were likely to fall that year: Ken Griffey, Jr., was on track to hit over 61 home runs; Yankee outfielder Paul O'Neill was getting hits so often that some sportswriters suggested he might be the man to equal or surpass Ted Williams' long-standing feat of batting at a .406 average.

Revenues from cable, broadcast, and licensing rights were more than healthy.

But the job action was called nevertheless. So the season came to an abrupt halt. The plug had been pulled. The lights went off.

At the beginning of negotiations, devotees were certain the opposing sides would settle their differences quickly. Games, they thought, would resume in a matter of days. However, as days turned into weeks, and one month into the next, even the most ardent of optimists had to admit that there was little hope for regular play to resume. In fact, it was in mid-September when they threw in the towel and declared there would not even be a World Series.

I am admittedly one among many major league fans who suffered something on the order of withdrawal symptoms when the strike began. (After all, we argue, what's summer without baseball?)

That's when the New Jersey Cardinals, a team brand-new to the ranks of minor league baseball, entered the picture.

For those not familiar with the sport, the minors are the proving ground of major league franchises. It's where the high school graduates and the college degree-holders get to test their abilities. It is a time for separating those who have enduring big league qualities from those whose meteoric rise turns out to be just that: a momentary flare in the heavens.

Skylands Park, where the Cardinals play, looks like something straight out of the movie *Field of Dreams*. The stadium's access road is a thin line of asphalt carved into the middle of a square mile of corn fields. Viewed from the outside, the stadium has the appearance of a round, red barn. From the inside, spectators have a spectacular view of giant maples and oaks, part of a wooded land lying just beyond the outfield wall. Bats — the flying variety — dart this way and that, high above the crowd, munching on insects, as wooden bats smack into horsehide below. By the time the plate umpire calls "Play ball!" the smell of new-mown hay has begun wafting over the ballpark. By the end of the game, the night mist has settled over center field.

Most importantly, a bunch of boys and girls — including the kids who are in their forties, fifties, sixties, and seventies — got to see great ball games in a year that the Big Boys of Astrodome, Fenway, and Chavez Ravine fame denied them the opportunity.

Unless you happen to live in the northern New Jersey area, you probably aren't familiar with names such as Brian Silva, Ossie Garcia, Aaron Gerteisen, and Steve Santucci. They were part of the young, upstart Cardinal team that won the New York-Penn League championship the first year they played, 1994.

But they very nearly missed the title. Interestingly, the same player who might have been the goat was credited with having lit the fire for their victory.

Rafael Robles was an up-and-coming third baseman. A good defensive player. An excellent batter. The only problem he had was after the regular season ended, when his team entered the play-offs. Robles couldn't get a hit. He couldn't even get the ball past the pitcher's mound. Eleven trips to the plate. Eleven outs.

In the final game, a crucial point arrived when everyone on the team needed to be especially sharp. On one play, the ball was hit sharply to the left side of the infield. Right at Robles. It took one hop, then another. He bent down, opened his glove, and got ready. The ball should have gone into the trap. The third baseman should have reached into his glove, grabbed the the ball, and made a quick throw to first. There should have been an out. The inning should have been over.

But it is said that baseball is a game of inches. And in that moment, when the play was over, no one knew it better than Rafael Robles. Because that's exactly what he missed by: a couple of inches. He positioned his glove just a little off target. The ball bounced off the heel of his glove instead of being trapped in its pocket. Instead of being the final out of the inning, a run was scored, and all hands were safe.

It so happened that in the Cardinals' half of the same inning, Robles' turn at bat came with two outs and the bases loaded. Everyone knew that he hadn't gotten a hit in the playoff games. Everyone knew the error he'd made was probably on his mind. Everyone knew he would likely make the third out.

So when Rafael Robles swung at a strike two pitch and hit a line drive straight at the shortstop, everyone in the stands assumed it would be caught. But it wasn't. The reason? Robles had smacked the ball so hard that it went sailing over the fielder's glove. Not by much. Just a couple of inches. But it was all that was needed.

His hit tied the game. And his team responded with so much enthusiasm that before the inning was over, they were ahead by four runs. They went on to win the game — and the championship.

Games are won and lost by inches:

- Errant throws that are tantalizingly close.
- Hits that just miss going out of the park.
- A tag that's made a split second too late.
- A diving attempt to catch the ball that drops just shy of the outstretched glove.

It reminds me of two words that someone once described as the saddest in our language: "almost persuaded."

Paul, the influential and persistent evangelist and missionary teacher of the gospel, not only told his own people, the Jews, about the Christ whom God had sent to save them from sin. He also convinced a reluctant Peter and James that Christ ought to be preached to the Gentiles — a people once considered to be forever beyond the pale of God's loving concern.

The apostle couldn't be stopped. He wouldn't shut up. In fact, he was arrested when he openly defied the law which stated that he could no longer promote his strange new faith. But detention only served to make him bolder.

While handcuffed to his jailor, Paul shared the message of the cross.

After he was shipwrecked with other prisoners, while waiting on the beach for another ship to pick them up, he testified about the compelling love of Christ to fellow inmates and to the Roman guards.

Years before, between one jail term and the next arrest, Paul had made his point about redemption in Christ, and the power of the cross, before the Judean king, Agrippa.

It was at that time, speaking with the high government official, that Paul pulled out all the stops and used his most convincing argument.

"First to those in Damascus, then to those in Jerusalem and in all Judea, and to the Gentiles also, I preached that they should repent and turn to God and prove their repentance by their deeds ... I have had God's help to this very day, and so I stand here and testify to small and great alike. I am saying nothing beyond what the prophets and Moses said would happen — that the Christ would suffer and, as the first to rise from the dead, would proclaim light to his own people and to the Gentiles" (Acts 26:20-23).

Now to his credit, King Agrippa did listen to what Paul said. He paid attention. He considered what was put before him.

Small wonder. For there in his presence was no prisoner begging for his freedom in abject contrition, but a man, already released from an everlasting destiny far worse than any earthly dungeon, proclaiming Christ Jesus as Savior and Lord without apology or hesitation.

However, in the end, Agrippa blew it. A brilliant argument from one of the best legal minds of the age, a detailed account of conversion from the mouth of one who had had a reputation as a persecutor of Christians but then had turned completely around in order to embrace the faith he once had hated, should have been enough to compel the king to kneel in awe before the risen Nazarene.

Agrippa came so near. He reached to within inches of the kingdom. But he fell so short of the mark. Ironically, he did comprehend (understand) the message, yet he did not apprehend (embrace or take to himself) it. You could say Agrippa failed because there was too much at stake —

- too much power,
- too much prestige,
- too much position,
- too much ego

— in short, too much of the king standing in the way of the Christ. So he concluded his discussions with the apostle by saying these sad words: "Almost thou persuadest me to be a Christian" (Acts 26:28, KJV).

Almost persuaded.

The human tendency of missing out by inches, the historic litany of "almost," later became a theme in Paul's letters. His apt description of sinners attempting to push, poke, prod, or otherwise shoehorn themselves into heaven by flaunting their own merit is probably drawn from observing archers. A group of them may have been having some fun one day at practice. They walked a considerable distance from the target. Then they drew back their bows and let the arrows fly.

The archers' aim was good. Their intent to hit the objective was evident. A graceful arc took each arrow toward the mark. And every single arrow landed nose-down in the ground, yards away from the goal.

The men almost did it. Their arrows almost reached the target. They almost got a prize for their skill.

But not quite.

In the same way, wrote Paul, "... [A]ll have sinned and fall short of the glory of God" (Romans 3:23). That little phrase, "have come up short," describes where all our own efforts will get us. It ought to give us a clear picture of humanity's status without a Redeemer.

It also ought to serve as a wake-up call for those who believe their affiliation with churches, parachurch groups, and religious organizations are equal to hitting the divine "bullseye." Because after all our years of service to the church, after all our volunteer hours spent as officers in the congregation or denomination, after all our time spent in the pew, God will not say certain things.

- He won't inquire as to how many minutes per week we have logged in patiently creating three-point sermons for the congregation.
- He won't ask how many minutes per week we have logged in patiently putting up with the preacher's overlong sermons.
- He won't ask on how many church-related relief agencies we served as local chairpersons.
- He won't ask us to give details of the anguish we experienced when elders who should have known better mispronounced Zerubbabel's name during the Bible study.

There are many things, we assure ourselves, that will impress God. Being a member of the right denomination has got to count for something, right? Being an officer will probably help the cause. Singing in the choir? That's a sure-fire way of getting into the heavenly chorus.

But then the Spirit of God breaks upon our neat and tidy speculations and says, "There is a way that seems right ... but its end is the way to death" (Proverbs 14:12).

A long time ago, it seemed right to a certain Judean king that he should hold onto his base of power, whether or not it meant running afoul of God's plan. It is one of the saddest stories in the Bible.

Word had reached the court that a certain child had been born within the Judean jurisdiction, in Bethlehem. This boy-child, according to a prophetic word, was to grow to be no ordinary man.

He was to be Light — "... [T]hose who lived in a land of deep darkness — on them light has shined" (Isaiah 9:2).

He was to be Redemption — "... [Y]ou are to name him Jesus, for he will save his people from their sins" (Matthew 1:21).

He was to be Ruler — "For the Lord your God is God of gods and Lord of lords ..." (Deuteronomy 10:17).

But Herod, though a puppet monarch, was still a tyrant. As a result, the religious council, not wanting to risk the king's displeasure, thought it prudent to be "yes men" rather than give even the slightest impression that they were disloyal.

We get a glimpse of his volatile personality when Matthew tells us that "King Herod ... was frightened, and all Jerusalem with him ..." (Matthew 2:3).

It seemed to the king's advisors that, given his unpredictable predisposition toward violent rages, it might not be the best time to remind him that the young child, which some visiting potentates inquired about, was prophesied in Holy Scriptures from the Torah to Micah as a King to rule over all kings, the Lord before whom all lords would bow.

So even though Bethlehem lies in the shadows of Jerusalem, they did not go. And though going there may have changed their minds about whom to serve, they did not try. And though making the attempt would have proven their everlasting joy, they did not risk the venture.

They missed the mark. By the shortest of distances. By the slimmest of errors. By the most simple of decisions.

But in spiritual matters, as in baseball, missing by inches is the same as missing by eternity.

By what you've done, have you hit God's mark? Only if "what you've done" includes faith.
- Not faith in general.
- Not faith in some kind of nebulous "Christmas ideal."
- Not faith in one or more of the causes that Christmas has come to represent — such as harmony, peace, and kindness.
- Not faith in yourself.
- Not faith for faith's sake alone.

Then faith in what? Or in whom? John the apostle gave the best Christmas sermon of all time when he wrote, "For God so loved the world that he gave his only Son, so that everyone who who believes in him may not perish but may have eternal life" (John 3:16).

In the end, God will ask each of us only one question. God will ask the writer of Christmas books and the readers. He will ask the rich and the poor, with no special preference given to either group. He will ask those who have conducted themselves like saints and those who have behaved like sinners.

God absolutely will not ask you about your ecclesiastical loyalties, whether you are a Baptist or Roman Catholic or Pentecostalist. God will not ask you about your political correctness. God will not ask you about your good deeds.

God will ask one question only. The answer you give will reveal whether or not in your lifetime you ever recognized and acknowledged that there is a way you could keep your life on target. "I am the way [said Jesus], and the truth, and the life. No one comes to the Father except through me" (John 14:6).

If you are off the mark, even in the slightest, you will get a one-way ticket out of the kingdom, a front row seat right outside the gates of heaven. You'll be forever looking in with longing, loneliness, and despair.

If you are on target, you'll be home. God be praised, your hitting the mark squarely has nothing to do with your ability — only his.

Here is that question: Did you put your whole trust in Christ Jesus, who died and rose again that you might live?

The apostle knew the Redeemer well. He knew Who had reached down, shaken him to the core, and set him straight. Paul knew Who had taken the arrow of his faltering faith and had winged it right to the center of the target. "[F]or I know the one in whom I have put my trust, and I am sure that he is able to guard until that day what I have entrusted to him" (2 Timothy 1:12).

In baseball you know what is going to happen: the crowd moans, the manager cringes, and the player kicks himself every time there is an "almost" experience. Almost in the glove. Almost a steal. Almost a tag. Almost out of the park. Almost a strikeout. Almost a win. And each miss is as good as a mile.

In life, it's not so easy to notice the reactions to what you think of Christmas, and the One born then. There's no one who can actually see you stepping up to the plate of faith, or taking care of the defense against sin. No one can see if you let Jesus take care of the aim and power departments. Or if you refuse to let him help. There's no coach shouting instructions. There's no gathering of fans to urge you on. There's no umpire to tell you when you're safe or out.

But life is just as much a series of "almosts" as baseball. And life is far more important than the game of baseball. Almost convinced. Almost won. Almost home.

Maybe you have played the game of life spectacularly up to this point. Singles and doubles based on neighborliness and helpful — even godly — deeds. But now you're in the field. The ball is headed your way. An inch one way or the other off dead center, and they'll be flashing the big *E* for "error." And you will lose it all.

Do you want to run the risk of missing out on the biggest win of your whole life? (Herod did. His advisors, too. Those who preferred an easy religion missed. Men and women who don't want God to challenge their way of life? They miss it. So do those who insist on celebrating Christmas without inviting Christ to the party.) Or would you prefer to have by your side the One who has already risked everything that you can have the whole ballgame? Because missing by inches is the same as missing by a mile.

10
Reunions

Luke 19:44

The older I get, the more I'm convinced that the best reunions are the ones that are unplanned.

Call me a social introvert, but I have never once responded to the invitation of my high school classmates to join them for those occasional gatherings — not even for the twenty-fifth, which I understand many consider an important milestone.

Don't misunderstand me. If you like that sort of thing, good for you! It's just that, personally, I'd rather avoid it. Maybe it's because the Clifton (New Jersey) Class of '66 to which I belonged had over a thousand in it, so any reunion has to be held in a ballroom roughly the size of an airplane hangar. Or maybe because the affair has so many details to consider, the planning's got to be started two or more years ahead of time. Everything has to be just so: the seating arrangements, the centerpieces, the lighting, the food, the service, the music, the speakers, the presentations.

By the time the doors open and the guests arrive, every move has been choreographed. Every minute's been planned. Every step has been laid out. Spontaneity? You've got to be kidding. There's no room for it anywhere.

Frankly, the sort of reunion I like to hear about is the kind that people never even dream could happen to them. The kind of reunion Bob Atkins had a few years ago.

At the time a 72-year-old retiree and resident of Lorain, Ohio, Atkins drove his wife to the local hospital for minor surgery, and sat down for a while in the waiting room. Almost immediately, he and another man, a stranger who was also awaiting word about his wife's condition, struck up a lively conversation.

65

In the course of their chat, the subject of military service came up. For Atkins, the matter hit a raw nerve. He had never quite gotten over the death of his best friend, Roy Stump. The two men had been in the Infantry during the Second World War, and were taking Holland back from the Germans a foot at time. Stump was walking just ahead of Atkins when he stepped on a land mine.

As he cradled his buddy's body, Atkins tried to stop the bleeding with a handkerchief. But the explosion had torn the left side of Stump's head away, and the medic who came along lingered only long enough to take the wounded soldier's dog tags. When the doctor left, Atkins knew the terrible truth: his friend Roy would not survive.

Now, over fifty years later, in a hospital waiting room, a flood of memory and sadness washed over him all over again. But the stranger interrupted Atkins' thoughts and silent grief as the two continued their conversation. "Anybody get hurt in your outfit?" he asked.

"Yeah," said Atkins. "Unfortunately. Good friend of mine, Roy Stump. Mine blew up in his face. Died right there on the field."

With that the other man got out his wallet, brought out his license and Army discharge papers and said, "Sorry to surprise you here, old buddy, but I didn't die!" It was Roy Stump, who not only did not perish, but fully recovered, went home, began a career, got married, and raised a family.

Unknown to either one of them, both men had moved to Lorain. They bought houses within five miles of each other, got gas at the same service station, and ate at the same diner at the same time of day. Stump remembers speaking to Atkins several times. The two always greeted each other cordially. But neither ever knew who the other was. Until that day at the hospital.

Since then, the two have been inseparable. They frequently have dinner at one another's homes. They have coffee and danish at the diner where they passed each other by so many times. And as you may have guessed, they talk endlessly. After all, when you think your best friend died a half century ago, you have a lot of catching up to do.

Long ago, a man and woman held a precious, dying comrade in their arms. They wept as they realized their loved one's life was ebbing away.

They themselves lay worn-out on a battlefield. They were bruised, broken, confused, and frightened. Their Enemy had used his best offense against them — a half-truth which made them first question, then doubt, and finally abandon a promise which, until that moment, had been their best defense.

You may know that postwar scene as "the fall." You know the fallen man and woman, too. Their names? Adam, Eve, parents of the human race, your forebears and mine. The crafty warlord is Satan.

And the friend who is wounded, bleeding, and dying is God's presence. God's friendship. God's fellowship. God's nearness. God's communion.

God had shared the secrets of creation, of the universe, of heaven and earth, with the man and woman. He had revealed truths to them which not even angels had been privileged to hear. He had made them, not to respond as computers are programmed to recall bits of typed-in data, but to freely converse with new ideas and new questions and new revelations.

As they lie in the dust, shell-shocked and trembling, rocking their friend as a mother would comfort her child, all that is now gone. Members of the Evac team move in, pause at the failing victim, shake their heads in sympathy, remove the dog tags — and move on.

And that is just where so many people think matters still stand: God's presence was taken away by a war crime, an act of deception, a sin, that was committed a long time ago; God's presence with the human race just died and turned into dust; truth, justice, and goodness disappeared and nothing was ever done about it since then.

If that is what you think has happened — nothing — then you'll pardon my saying it but —

Where have you been?

What have you been doing?

And what have you been reading?

The true story of two army buddies illustrates the condition of so many people. Are you among them? There are so many who really don't know what an earlier generation used to call the imminence of God. Are you among them? Contemporary Americans don't seem to have a clue when it comes to the presence of God in the world. If they think of God at all, they believe his last appearance in the universe was at the dawn of time. The words of the Bible really fit them: "Thou knewest not the time of thy visitation" (Luke 19:44, KJV).

Are you among them?

Do you know that God lives nearby? Have you not seen that he's a neighbor of yours? Are you aware that he was never far away to begin with? But do you realize that God never came so close to you as he did when, as Scripture says, "And the Word became flesh and lived among us ..." (John 1:14). That is the message and the miracle of Advent: reunion.

- God coming to the earth to heal the severed relationship. Reunion.
- God making right what had been wrong for so many years. Reunion.
- God restoring wholeness of heart where there had been only brokenness of spirit. Reunion.

And, like the best reunions, that one — the birth of Jesus — was filled with spontaneity. Not from God's perspective, but from ours. God was planning it for a long time. But as far as we were concerned, there were going to be no more surprises ... no more visitations from heaven ... no more words ... no more actions ... no more conversation or communion with the Creator.

So when a heavenly messenger split the night sky to announce the holy birth: Wow, what a party!

And what about you? Just when you are good and lonely, just when you're on the edge of giving yourself over to despair, just when you are ready to say what you have felt for so long, that God has left forever ... he comes.

God comes on a silent night to announce that the reunion party is about to begin.

He comes to tell you the patient has not died.

He comes to give you the truth: The Lord of Hosts is both Creator and Friend ... the Judge of sin and the Savior of sinners ... wholly Other and wholly God-With-Us ... one whose home is in heaven and in the believing human heart.

Do you know this God? If you do — if you can recognize the Almighty in the face of Jesus Christ — then let the reunion begin!

11
The Quiet Man

Matthew 1:19

*[Mary's] husband Joseph, being a righteous man and
unwilling to expose her to public disgrace, planned to
dismiss her quietly. But just when he had resolved to do
this, an angel of the Lord appeared to him in a dream
and said, "Joseph, Son of David, do not be afraid to
take Mary as your wife, for the child conceived in her
is from the Holy Spirit. She will bear a son, and you are
to name him Jesus ..." When Joseph awoke, he did as
the angel of the Lord commanded him; he took [Mary]
as his wife (Matthew 1:19-21, 24).*

Simplicity is the thread that attaches God's help to our need.
Wise are God's servants who learn to stitch straight lines.

Preachers often lose sight of that fact. They tend to weave un-
necessarily intricate theological patterns which entangle the feet
of those looking for God, and strangle their understanding of what
is really an easily-understood gospel. Somtimes it takes nothing
more than a plain, unadorned act of love to clear away the web so
the thread can be seen.

The late Harry Rogers was a self-effacing sort who was easily
embarrassed when any accolades were given him for what he did.
The same can be said of his widow, Betty. But I think it's time to
say that the Rogerses performed a ministry that is one of the most
profound I have ever encountered.

It also happens to be one of the simplest and most quiet. And it
reminds me of a man whose story in the Bible is unique in that not
one word he uttered is quoted, yet he has influenced generations as
if what he said filled volumes.

To a freshman at a small liberal-arts college in the hills of north-western Pennsylvania, Dr. Harry Rogers' method of teaching New Testament Greek made a considerable impact. It is something that I've never forgotten. Before any of us knew how to fully decipher the Greek alphabet, before we knew anything of *Koine* idioms, before we knew the intricacies of parsing — from the first day of Greek 101, we began translating the Gospel according to John, from the first verse of chapter one:

Εν αρξη ην ο λογοσ, και ο λογοσ ην προσ τον θεον, και θεοσ ην ο λογοσ.

(In the beginning was the Word, and the Word was with The God, and God was the Word.)

Dr. Rogers of Grove City College had a theory, that something worth doing is worth pursuing one hundred percent. Plunge right in. Don't hesitate. Even if it goes against the current of conventional wisdom. Even if it doesn't square with tried-and-true methods that have been used for long periods of time.

What was true of his standards in the classroom was also true of his home life. As vigorously and exuberantly as he taught, Harry Rogers played. He loved railroading. He had train paraphernalia all over. He had shelves, stacks, boxes full of timetables, dating from goodness-knows-when, culled from goodness-knows-where. He was always sending away for updated versions.

The same thing can be said of Betty Rogers. When she worked, she took the job seriously. When it was time for recreation, she had fun! I remember that it was just about the time we pre-seminary types were getting just a wee grim about our studies that we'd get an invitation to go to Dr. and Mrs. Rogers' house. We would talk. We would tell jokes. We would play parlor games. The kind of activities more reminiscent of the late nineteenth century than two-thirds of the way through the twentieth.

But it was just what we needed! And at just the right time. Betty had an uncanny knack of knowing exactly when to tell us to "lighten up." I guess it was part of her ministry to people she thought of as friends, not just students. (Incidentally, if you are ever curious, please drop me a line and ask me what "This Is a Dog ..." is all about.)

Harry and Betty Rogers also sent out Christmas cards. Betty still does. That in itself is not really unusual. What is different is the number of cards that are mailed. If my math is correct, by now it must be hovering somewhere near 1,200. What is also different is how the cards are prepared. Every day of the year, the Rogerses randomly selected three or four cards that had been sent to them the previous Christmas. Betty carries on that tradition.

What did this dear couple do with the cards?
• They read the message.
• They thought of the individual, couple, or family represented by the card.
• They prayed for them.

Harry and Betty prayed specifically and intentionally for their health, their spiritual life in Christ, their joy in the Lord. Then, and only then, was the card signed and the envelope addressed.

It was a quiet ministry, silent to all but God and themselves, but it was a ministry nonetheless. It continues to be just that.

What difference does it make? What possible need is met in this high-tech age by receiving a Christmas card that the widow of a retired professor has prayed over? Just ask those who have said it was just what the doctor ordered, to realize that someone had expended the care, time, and prayer in order to express love. Ask those whose sagging souls were summoned from the shadows by the Spirit of God who flew to their side on the wings of intercession.

It is a simple, straight thread of prayer linking God to one who needs God.

In this age, we have been conditioned to give special attention to the boisterous, the showy, the "glitzy," and the just plain noisy. We have been allured by piercing decibels — the louder something is said or sung, the better and more truthful it must be. Or so we have been told.

Yet God has always spoken most eloquently in the silence.

As a result of our patterning, we tend to miss a great deal that the Lord has in store for us. We fail to stop and listen in the pauses of life — the quiet times — the spaces between one crisis and the next. We're grim, we're short, and we're ill-tempered.

Consider: the incarnate Word of God — Jesus Christ — was given in the still of the night in a quiet, obscure village in a corner of the Judean landscape; he was greeted, mind you, not by the official leadership of his day nor by their representatives, but by the silent reverence of awe-struck, adoring shepherds who knew that something wonderful had happened to them and to the whole world.

Several weeks earlier, in obedience to both the civil authorities and the irresistible will of God, Joseph of Nazareth packed up his bags and, with Mary his beloved, headed for Bethlehem, where they would be registered for the census.

> *All went to their own towns to be registered. Joseph also went from the town of Nazareth in Galilee to Judea, to the city of David called Bethlehem, because he was descended from the house and family of David. He went to be registered with Mary, to whom he was engaged and who was expecting a child (Luke 2:3-5).*

If you look for a description of God's call to serve written by Joseph, you won't find it. If you search for words of wisdom he may have shared with those of his home synagogue in Nazareth, you won't find them. If you hope to find something comparable to Mary's song of joy, but spoken by Joseph, your pursuit will be in vain.

All we know of Joseph is that he was a righteous man, a man who loved Mary very much, a man who was fiercely protective of his soon-to-be wife. A man who knew what it was to have doubts.

A man who knew the triumph of faith.

A man who knew that God often speaks most eloquently in the silence.

Joseph embodies the principle that the best theologies are not necessarily the most complicated, but the simple ones that show where to find God's strength in the moment of crisis. A theology that falls back, not on law but on faith. In Nazareth, had Joseph become entangled with the web of legalism, he likely would have let Mary fall victim to stoning, or else headed the line of her accusers. Later, in Bethlehem, had Joseph been more concerned with the form of his "righteous" and "just" behavior than the behavior itself, by the time he got around to helping Mary she would have already given birth to the Redeemer alone, helpless and miserable.

Joseph had a quiet ministry. We can only speculate as to what he said to his beloved, because not one word is recorded in Scripture. But because he is noted as one who did what was good and just, we know that what he did for Mary was exactly what she needed. He prayed for her. He begged God's strength for her. He implored the Almighty that she might be given comfort in her hour of need. And he asked that his love might be enough, that it would see her through.

It did.

When was the last time you caught hold of the simple thread? There are books on pure theology written in scholarly terms so complex, an academic would have a hard time getting past the preface. Then there are books which are a curious combination of theological musings and self-help. Into a third category you can put works that are closer to New Age human potential ritual and hype than theology.

Unfortunately, they all fail to live up to their intended goal. And what, after all, is the goal of theology except to assist the reader to understand the Bible and the God who authored it?

Maybe in your life there is some Joseph of Nazareth, or some Harry or Betty Rogers, whose theology is utterly simple. (One illustrious seminary professor, when asked by a student what he considered the greatest theological statement, is reported to have said, "Jesus loves me, this I know, for the Bible tells me so.") What he or she has done was intended to help you out of some problem or rut. But you have rejected it because it doesn't "fit" into your stereotype of what is theology and what is not. Maybe you have the notion that great theologies have to come packaged in full-color slip jackets and hand-sewn hardcovers. Maybe you think they have to have the imprimatur of some mainline denomination.

And maybe you equate *simple* with *silly*.

If you do, I would like to offer the following axioms. They deal with those who have more than their share of problems but don't know where to turn. They are decidedly simple, but they have proven helpful to more than a few people:

- The Bible is a book that tells of imperfect, sinful persons.
- The gospel is a story that tells of God's mercy.
- There isn't a person alive who doesn't need help.
- You can't be helped if you don't admit it.
- Compassion isn't a crutch.
- Somewhere, someone wants to give you compassion.
- True love doesn't cost a cent.
- God's grace is true love, and you don't owe him anything.
- Christmas is not a sweet, sappy, saccharine story. It is not a story to be dragged out and dusted off one quick season of the year.

Christmas is a powerful story, a story of true love, the truest love that ever existed. Salvation's power, love's source, came in the quiet and unpresuming anonymity of a profoundly simple birth on a silent night that was made holy by heaven touching earth, the divine coming among us, God dwelling among us, Emmanuel.

And thus, the Almighty works through all the Josephs, Marys, Harrys, Bettys, and the rest of those quiet folks who know that simplicity is the thread that attaches God's help to our need.

12
Justice

Romans 5:6-7

Let me say from the outset that I am not ashamed to profess my love for the land of my birth. I'll never deny the fact that my heart swells when they play "The Star-Spangled Banner." I can tell you without blinking an eye that America is still the land of opportunity where bold ideas are both dreamed and lived out, and (would you believe it?) the oldest surviving experiment in democracy.

However, "it ain't poifect!" Although the government safeguards our freedoms, the government also makes mistakes. Submitted for your consideration: a letter, mailed just a few years ago from the Internal Revenue Service, which stated that our bank account had been frozen, sent shivers up our backs (no pun intended).

Seems that someone somewhere made an incorrect data entry. Made it appear that I earned a whole bunch more than I really did. *You owe us a pile of dough,* they said. *Pay up. Oh, and by the way, we're tacking on some hefty penalties and interest.*

Folks in the church I serve know their pastor is no math wiz or accountant. I panic when the Treasury Department says they're right and I'm wrong. So I sought help from an attorney. In the end, everything was squared away. My blood pressure's nearly back to normal. And I can sleep again.

It occurs to me now that at some time after the initial shock of "What are we going to do?" had worn off, the wave of disbelief began to be replaced by a profound sense of having been wronged. We were angry. We believe in the United States. We pay our taxes. How could our own government do this to us? Why don't they go after the real deadbeats, those who work but don't pay IRS anything, or those who never fill out a 1040? We want justice done! (Can you relate?)

Then it struck me: if a human being can experience feelings of injustice, how much more does God! God knows me — my mind, my heart, my intent, my inclination — better than anyone else. God knows when I skirt the truth in order to avoid embarrassment. *Dan, you've lied.* God knows when I look at the stats and note that some guy I graduated with is now pastoring a 3000-member church in Albuquerque. *Dan, you're coveting what your neighbor's got.* God knows when I fail to be a loving husband or a caring father. *Dan, you are a thief of the joy your family may have had otherwise.* And I wince, because I know it's all true: "Thou shalt not steal ... Thou shalt not bear false witness ... Thou shalt not covet ..." (Deuteronomy 5:19-21).

Know what? You have the same problem. No, I don't mean that you've lied, coveted, or stolen the same way I have. But in one way or another, you too have broken the Law. The moral code of God. The Ten Commandments. Or the two great commandments: "You shall love the Lord your God ... [and] you shall love your neighbor as yourself" (Mark 12:30, 31). Or the law of mercy: "Forgive, and you will be forgiven" (Luke 6:37). Or the law of compassion: "[J]ust as you did it to one of the least of these who are members of my family, you did it to me" (Matthew 25:40).

Every infraction of God's set of regulations — be it great or ever so small — is not merely an "oops!" in the midst of an otherwise placidly pleasant relationship to God. It is a sin. A rebellious act. A thumbing of the nose in God's face.

It is a direct affront to him, an injustice that cries out for justice. Scripture makes this stinging indictment about you and me:

> *... [Deeds] of violence are in their hands. Their feet run to evil ... The way of peace they do not know, and there is no justice in their paths ... Therefore justice is far from us, and righteousness does not reach us ... For our transgressions before you are many, and our sins testify against us ... So justice is turned back ... truth stumbles in the public square, and uprightness cannot enter ... The Lord saw it, and it displeased him that there was no justice (Isaiah 59:6-7, 8, 9, 12, 14, 15).*

The point is that if we, who are human, want every wrong righted, every infraction of the law met with swift punishment, and every injustice corrected by retribution or restitution, how much more does God! It is God's laws that are broken and flaunted every time the sinner sins. Know what? When you tell a half-truth to your spouse, you lie to God. When you steal answers on an exam, you cheat God. When you lash out in violence against another, you slap God. When you revolt against moral law, you oppose God.

I've often wondered if some church leaders who've made it a habit of crying out for God's justice to be done have really looked at what "justice" means. It strikes me that if they did, they wouldn't be calling for God's justice. They would be calling out for God's mercy.

If God were to mete out his justice on all sinners (you'll pardon the vernacular), we'd all be toast ... history ... swiss cheese ... in the dumpster. Why? Because God makes no distinction between "pretty good sinners" and "really rotten" sinners: "... [A]ll have sinned and fall short of the glory of God" (Romans 3:23).

Wait a minute, Dan! Are you suggesting that the guy who bilks some little old lady out of millions and then underpays his taxes by hundreds of thousands is in the same boat as another guy who helps little old ladies across the street and has never underreported a dime of income?

Yep. Except actually, it isn't I who suggests it. It's God who flatly states it.

So you're in deep water. Up to your neck. And sinking fast. That's why you don't need justice.

You need an advocate.

In a courtroom, the accused is represented by an attorney who pleads a case for her client. She is his advocate, in that she speaks on his behalf to try to convince the court of some set of facts. She says to the judge, "Judge, the accused is innocent of the charges which have been leveled against him. I am convinced of this because of the following circumstances."

The attorney then proceeds to give the reasons why she believes the accused man should not be found guilty of the crime.

But you need an advocate of a different kind. Why? Because the Word of God, and God himself, have already pronounced you guilty of sin. The advocate you need is one who once said to the Almighty, "Judge, since my client is guilty of being a sinner, and you have already prescribed the sentence — 'For the wages of sin is death' (Romans 6:23) — I will pay the fine ... I will suffer the penalty ... I am willing to be convicted of the crime of sin ... I will die in place of this sinner. Will this satisfy your justice? Will it be in your eyes, Judge, that this person has committed no crime, has performed no wrong, has done no sin?"

And the Almighty Judge said, with no little difficulty, because the Advocate happened to be the Judge's Son: "I will accept your offer, and it will satisfy my justice. Your client will live, because he has put trust in your ability to represent and save."

> *Surely he has borne infirmities and carried our diseases ... he was wounded for our transgressions, [and] crushed for our iniquities; upon him was he punishment that made us whole, and by his bruises we are healed. All we like sheep have gone astray ... and the Lord has laid on him the iniquity of us all (Isaiah 53:4, 5-6).*

Do you know the reason the Son made such a decision, such an offer? It wasn't your money; you don't have enough. It wasn't your innate goodness; you don't have any. It wasn't your charm; even the devil has that, and it doesn't do him a lick of good.

The only reason God the Son planned to be your Advocate is because of his own love. What a precedent was established! (Incidentally, it is a precedent that has never been equalled.) As Paul the apostle remarked in astonishment:

> *Indeed, rarely will anyone die for a righteous person — though perhaps for a good person someone might actually dare to die. But God proves his love for us in that while we still were sinners Christ died for us (Romans 5:7-8).*

But love — yes, even God's love — is an empty thing unless there is both a bestower and a receiver. Stories of unreturned human love make for the saddest of all literary works. And cases of unrequited divine love make for the deepest tragedies of all.

Did you recognize this as a Christmas story? You should. At Christmas, when our thoughts turn toward gifts ... at Christmas, when our hearts turn toward love ... at Christmas, when our souls turn toward hope ... that is when our whole selves ought to be turned toward the Christ.

That humanity the creature was prone to sin ... that Jesus the Son was eager to offer ... and that God the Father was willing to accept ... that is the meaning of Christmas. But that you the sinner be ready to receive its gift ... that is the hope of Christmas.

13
Nobility

Revelation 17:14

Joe Dean is retired now. However, time was, not too many years ago, that he was chief steward at the exclusive and prestigious Baltusrol Country Club in New Jersey.

In case you don't know what a good country club steward does, he's the guy who makes you feel as if you're the only person who matters. He rolls out the red carpet of hospitality, then guides you across it. He knows your last name. First and middle names, too. And if you have a nickname that you hate, he will never, ever repeat it to anyone. He notes your birthday on the calendar, and sees to it that the baker prepares a little cake in your honor. (And if he can sing, you'll get a rendition of "Happy Birthday To You," too.) He will always ask you about your wife, your husband, your children, your mom, and your dad.

Dean was such a steward, and more. He remembered details. Insignificant things to some, but important to the guests. How you like a twist of lime in your cola. How you detest anything but black cut tea with your lightly toasted, unbuttered English muffin. How you prefer the table with the view of the brook and not of the fountain.

He kept secrets well, too. Golf handicaps — the real ones. The number of desserts eaten. Amount of alcohol consumed. That sort of thing.

He left his long career as steward a happy, secure man. And although he once rubbed elbows with them, Joe Dean now loves to sit back and tell stories about conversations he had with the elite, rich, and powerful. You won't read about them in some "kiss-and-tell" paperback. Joe just likes to reminisce.

They had a special visitor some time ago, he says. It seems that the Prince of Wales visited Baltusrol a few decades back. The highborn guest knew of Dean's prominence as a steward and had asked for him by name. After some animated conversation, the Prince of Wales leaned toward his host as if he were about to utter something utterly confidential. Joe inclined his ear obligingly, just in time to hear the prince say, "By the way, my father was the king."

Interesting. A strange comment, according to Joe. " 'My father was the king'?" he says. "As if there were any question about it!"

Well put, Mr. Dean. True nobility doesn't go about dropping regal names. It doesn't flaunt its position. Nor does it explain itself. It doesn't have to. It simply is. Those with a shaky understanding of their own inheritance may have to parade titles about. But those of real royal stuff know who they are.

The name Herod was both feared and hated by many Jews in the ancient Middle East. It represented a family of tyrants. It represented a regime of cruelty. It represented, for the people, a worse oppression than Rome, because the royal family they should have been able to trust sold them out to their captors. Scripture doesn't mention it, but I guess name-dropping was part of Herod's daily diet of self-admiration: "Oh, by the way, did I tell you? My father was king, too."

And Herod was jealous. To the point of paranoia. Members of his court, members of his staff, members of his family, no one was above his suspicious and watchful eye.

Given his extreme jealousy, it is no wonder that when a certain caravan from east of Judea arrived at Herod's palace one day, the king was more than a little upset. It was a group of royals who had stopped by. That, in itself, was no cause for alarm. Potentates were a regular feature in the capital city. But why they had come to Jerusalem — that was a big problem. It seems they hadn't dropped in to see Herod. They weren't there to have tea and cake. They didn't come on a diplomatic quest. They wouldn't even stay the night. They had come to get some directions, nothing more. Then they'd be on their way. Directions to where? Or, better stated, to whom? To a place where a child had been born. A baby boy.

A new star had appeared, they said. They were puzzled about it. Couldn't find anything like it in the astronomical maps. Wasn't in their astrological charts, either. So they began pouring over some old scientific manuscripts, literature, and religious works. And in the middle of an old Judean prophecy, they found what they were looking for. If there were an Oriental equivalent of "Wow!" they used it when they started to read.

[A] star shall come out of Jacob, and a scepter shall rise out of Israel (Numbers 24:17).

But you, O Bethlehem of Ephrathah, who are one of the little clans of Judah, from you shall come forth for me one who is to rule in Israel, whose origin is from of old, from ancient days (Micah 5:2).

As shepherds seek out their flocks when they are among their scattered sheep, so I will seek out my sheep. I will rescue them from all the places to which they have been scattered on a day of clouds and thick darkness. I will bring them out from the peoples and gather them from the countries ... (Ezekiel 34:12-13).

A shoot shall come out from the stump of Jesse, and a branch shall grow out of his roots ... the root of Jesse shall stand as a signal to the peoples (Isaiah 11:1, 10).

To whom does a scepter belong? A king. What kind of person rules over Israel? A king. What kind of shepherd can bring exiles out of countries where they have been scattered? A king. Who serves as an ensign for the people? A king. So who would pose the greatest threat ever mounted against the fraud and corruption perpetuated in the Herod lineage? Right. A king. A king in David's line. A good and just king. A king chosen by God.

So when Scripture says, "... King Herod ... was frightened, and all Jerusalem [its religious leaders] with him ..." (Matthew 2:3),

85

it's not talking about a minor disturbance within the royal compound! Herod was livid. Herod was at stroke level. Herod was fit to be tied. Herod threatened his advisors with beatings or worse if they didn't give him the right information, and quickly. Remember: Herod was a despot and a jealous man. A man filled with himself. A man impressed with titles. A man who probably loved to hear himself say, "My father was king, you know."

And now, a man desperate to preserve his throne. Guard against all pretenders. Kill any child who might grow up and march against the crown. Even if the Child turned out to be the Son of the heavenly King, the most high God.

I'm sure you are familiar with the rest of the story. Herod dispatches the Temple guards into the Judean countryside. He orders that all males two years old and younger are to be executed. But the wise men inform Jesus' parents of the impending disaster, and they flee to safety in Egypt.

Those like Herod who have a shaky understanding of their own standing may have to parade their titles and their power about. But those of true nobility — like Jesus of Nazareth — don't go around dropping regal names, theirs or anyone else's.

Jesus didn't have to flaunt his position. He didn't have to explain himself. He didn't have to give people a set of complicated directions to find him. He didn't have to. He, simply, was the King. He knew who he was.

And, to this day, those who are wise enough to look — will find him.

14
Christmas Is ...

Revelation 7:12

The more time passes, the more we realize that preparation for Christmas occupies our attention for a much greater part of the year than a few fleeting days in late December.

It is now commonplace to see, in our chain hardware stores and discount centers, where late September's row upon row of fertilizers, lawn mowers, wicker furniture, and pool supplies had stood, early October's display of — what? Rakes? Pruning shears? Leaf baggers? No. Christmas trees, lights, ornaments, and cards. And summer breezes are still wafting about us when the radio blares forth a timely (?) message, "With the holidays fast approaching ..."

Well, it's true that we are a lot busier now. Less time to waste than ever. Two- and three-salary households are more the rule than the exception. So we must seize the early moment while we can; we can ill afford the luxury of waiting until the week before Christmas to begin our making ready.

But make ready for what? Or for whom? We push Christmas along at such a fevered pitch that we tend to push Christmas away. At least what Christmas is.

So this year, let us remember these things:

Christmas is forever a "silent night" amidst days of discordant and shrieking claims. *Christmas is* Light piercing boldly into the darkness in spite of the night's every attempt to quench it.

Christmas is a simple message to a cultured age (and let us take heed, lest we ever forget that "sophisticated" is often mere artificiality, while simplicity can be utterly profound).

Christmas is the fluttering of angel wings just above the plodding of human feet. *Christmas is* the announcement of burdens lifted. *Christmas is* news of great gladness to replace unbearable sadness.

87

Christmas is for the young and the old, the scholar and the unschooled, the powerful and the powerless. *Christmas is* the fulfillment of age-old longings for peace, forgiveness, and fellowship.

Christmas is no magical restorative in itself for either sorrow, strife, or loneliness, but *Christmas is* the signature of One that had been born who would deal decisively with every one of those human maladies.

Christmas is singing the tried-and-true carols with gusto and even attempting an unfamiliar tune with good humor. *Christmas is* hearing the love of the Almighty in the cry of a Babe. *Christmas is* seeing the compassion of heaven in the streets of Bethlehem.

Christmas is all that is good and noble in the heart of God. *Christmas is* not for the perfect and morally impeccable among us, but for the grimy, wretched sinner.

Christmas is, above all the noise and glitter of celebration, the birthday of One those with clear eyes of faith call Redeemer, God, and King. *Christmas is* joy "in the city of David," and in a thousand thousand other cities, for unto *us* "is born a Savior — Christ the Lord!"

15
Davy

Luke 2:10-12

A Children's Christmas Story

Davy counted his change one last time before zipping up his thick coat, pulling his woolen ski cap over his head, and putting on his warm gloves. He smiled. Just as he had figured: 25 dollars. Not a penny more and not a penny less. Twenty-five dollars that he had earned.

In February, after the big blizzard, Mrs. MacGregor, who lived down the street, was not able to go to the store for milk and bread. She had asked Davy to go for her, and gave him a five-dollar bill to pay for the food.

When he delivered what Mrs. MacGregor had wanted, he gave her the two dollars and five cents that was her change. But Mrs. MacGregor refused to take it. Instead, she smiled and said, "No, Davy, you've earned that money by trudging through all that snow and slush for me. Please keep it. And thank you very much for your help."

During the summer, Davy had helped the librarians in town sort a lot of books. Two young men, who thought they were just playing a practical joke, had broken into the library one night and mixed up all the books in two whole stacks of bookshelves before the police arrived and arrested them. Over the next few days, Davy and a girl in his class put the books back on the shelves in the right order, so people could find them and use them.

After they were done, Dr. Stelmeyer, the head librarian, gave one envelope to Sylvia and one to Davy. Inside each envelope was a brand new ten-dollar bill and a brand new five-dollar bill. Dr. Stelmeyer had written a note which said, "All the librarians at the South Middleton Public Library want to thank you for taking the time to help us rearrange books after the recent break-in. Yours sincerely, Ms. Laura Michaels, Mr. John LaGrange, and Dr. Elizabeth Stelmeyer."

Later that same year, in the fall, Davy's father had fallen from a ladder. Mr. Blackman had set the ladder against the house, just outside Davy's second-floor bedroom; he wanted to clean out the gutters before winter came. But a big gust of wind came along. The ladder — and Davy's dad — came crashing down. Mr. Blackman's right leg was broken, and his right wrist was terribly sprained. "Davy," he said several days after the accident, "I always do the leaf-raking, but not this year, I'm afraid! Will you do it? Because it is hard work, and something that I do not expect you to do until you are older," he explained, "I will give you several dollars after the job is done." Davy agreed.

After all the leaves were raked, Davy's dad gave his son a five-dollar bill and a ten-dollar bill — fifteen dollars all together. Now Davy had 27 dollars and five cents. After he bought a Mini-Machine AT-3 attack fighter and an almond chocolate candy bar, he had exactly 25 dollars.

It was money that he had saved all year long. And he knew just what he was going to do. He was going to the store to get Christmas presents for his family. And that is exactly what Davy did.

For his sister Krystal he bought a new brown wallet. The one she had used for years was falling apart.

For his sister Shannon he bought a roll of film. She was always using her camera to get pictures of her friends.

For his mom he bought a pair of navy blue shoes at the BuyMore discount shoe store. Because she walked so much, Mom always needed an extra pair of shoes.

And for his dad he bought a #3 Philips screwdriver. Dad said his #2 screwdriver was just a little too small sometimes, and would slip.

After Davy was done buying the last thing on his Christmas list, he had 85 cents left. He bought five chocolate mints. He figured he would tape one mint on each of the four presents. He ate the fifth one.

Before long, it was Christmas Eve. After going to the late night church service on Christmas Eve with their parents, Davy and his sisters ran home as quickly as they could. They burst into the warm house and turned on the lights. Davy sat down in the big comforable chair. Shannon and Krystal went into the kitchen. A few minutes later, their mom and dad joined them.

In the living room, under the brightly-lit Christmas tree, were what seemed to be a hundred packages, all in paper wrapping of green, red, and white. The family decided they would open their gifts right then and there.

Davy saw a small stack of presents just in front of the tree. It was the wallet, the film, the shoes, and the tool he had bought for his family. He smiled as, first his dad, then Shannon, next Krystal, and finally his mom, opened the neatly-wrapped gifts. Each of them thanked Davy for his thoughtfulness.

Then Mom said, "Now, Davy, we have some things for you!" She pointed to a number of presents that were in front of the tree, just to the left of where he was sitting on the carpet.

The pile was big. In fact, to Davy, it was huge! There must have been eight — no, a dozen — packages, all with his name on them! One of the tags said, "Merry Christmas. To Davy. From Shannon." Three boxes had tags that said, "Christmas Joy! To Davy. Hugs 'n' kisses from Krystal." The rest of the presents had tags that said, "Peace at Christmastime. To Davy. Love, Mom and Dad."

Davy stared. Davy swallowed hard. Davy thought and thought. Davy measured the pile with his eyes. Davy frowned. There was no doubt. Next to what he had given to his parents and sisters — why, what his family had given to him was a skyscraper!

After a minute, he said, in a kind of thoughtful and drawn-out way, "No-o-o-o, I don't think so."

It was Shannon who was the first to speak. "Take a chill, Davy! Whaddya mean, 'I don't think so'? Are you saying you don't like our Christmas presents?" Mom was upset, too. "What's going on, David John?" she asked.

"I don't know, Mom," Davy answered. Turning to Shannon, he said, "It's not that I hate what you guys gave me. I haven't even opened anything, so I don't know what's inside." Then turning to the whole family, he explained, "It's just that you've given me so much, and I've given you so little. I can't accept your presents!"

Well, no sooner had he exclaimed, "I can't accept your presents," than a deep rumble shook the entire house. No one in the room seemed to notice. He was just about to say, "Hey! Didn't you hear that?" But before he could open his mouth, an amazing change came over everything.

- The big Christmas tree just vanished.
- A thousand colored lights which he had seen shimmering through the living room window disappeared.
- A string of Christmas cards which had hung over and beside the front door was ... gone!
- A CD of "Silent Night" and other Christmas songs which had been playing could no longer be heard.

It was very quiet — too quiet. And the presents? Every last one of them was missing. No red, green, and white wrapping paper. No bows. No tags. Davy shouted, "Where are the presents I gave everybody?" "'Presents'?" his dad said, as if he had never heard the word before. "What's 'presents'?"

Davy was annoyed. "You know, Dad! Things we buy for each other and give at Christmas." Now Dad was annoyed. "There you go again, David John, using words that nobody understands," he said. "What's this 'Cris-mus' you're talking about? I never heard of it before." Mom said, "I'll bet it's one of those new holidays — you know, the kind some card company dreamed up, like Bosses' Day or Grandparents' Day, so they could make more money. If it is, you can just forget about it, because I don't want any part of it."

Davy couldn't believe his ears! His mom and dad didn't know what Christmas was? As he was thinking of something to say, he saw a faint glow where the Christmas tree had stood just a couple of minutes before. It quickly grew brighter, and took the shape of ... could it be? Yes, it was an angel!

The other people in the room didn't see him. They seemed to be frozen in place, as when somebody presses "Pause" on a video player. "Davy," the angel said firmly. Davy was scared. "Uh ... yeah?" he finally managed to croak.

"Davy, there isn't any Christmas celebration. There aren't any presents. There's no tree, either. Or lights. Or carols. Because a long, long time ago, the people I visited in Bethlehem — the

92

shepherds — refused to accept God's gift that I had been sent to announce.

"I shared the good news with them. I said, 'I bring you wonderful tidings ... This day, in the city of David, a Savior [is born for you]. He is Christ the Lord ... You will find him lying in a manger.'

"But they answered, 'We will not go.'

"I was amazed. I couldn't believe what I was hearing! I said, 'Why won't you see the wonderful thing that God has done for you?' The shepherds said, 'We cannot receive God's Son, because we are poor. Don't you see? God has given us so much, and we can give him so little.'

"Davy, do you understand? There is no Christmas, because people just like you would not reach out and take the gift. The gift that was theirs to take. The gift that was free. The gift of love. Now it's too late."

As the angel and the light surrounding him began to grow dim, he put a hand softly on Davy's shoulder and said sadly, "It's late. It's late."

Davy awoke to the gentle sound of his mother's voice. She had put her hand on his shoulder, and was saying, "It's late. Maybe you'd like to wait until morning to open our Christmas gifts." Davy's eyes snapped open. Christmas gifts? The tree! It was still there, just where it belonged! So were the cards, the lights. And ...

And the little nativity scene. He'd forgotten about that! Little figures of Mary and Joseph and the baby Jesus.

And the shepherds. He had never noticed before that the artist who had sculpted the tiny shepherd figures made them so their hands were reaching out, palms up, as if they were about to take something.

"The Gift," Davy whispered. "They're taking the Gift. Even though they're going to receive everything and don't have gold, frankincense, or myrrh or anything to give in return, they're taking the Gift."

Turning his head back from the tableau, a broad smile grew over his entire face as he said, "No, Mom, I really think now — right now — is the time to give ... and receive."

16
Names

Matthew 1:21

One day in the middle of spring a few years ago, one of our elders found himself on a collision course with the clock. (Only the name has been changed to protect the embarrassed!) He had just exited a meeting with several alumni at his alma mater on a day that also featured the wedding of his cousin. The church where the bride and groom were to be married was distant by about an hour's worth of driving.

By the time our elder and his wife arrived at the motel where they were to change from casual clothing into more formal, the wedding was less than a half-hour away. But he didn't know if he had found the right lodging, so he bolted from the car and ran into the lobby to get the information. "I need to know right away," he puffed, "if this is the Radisson where my wife and I have reservations."

"You're Nate Houston," said the smiling manager, "and yes, you've come to the right place. In fact, we've been expecting your arrival. Here is your key."

"That's great," said the elder, as he ran out the door. He reappeared a second later. "But tell me, since hundreds of people come through here every day, how do you know who I am?"

The young woman grinned. "Simple," she said, "you're the only one who's come in today wearing a name tag!"

I wonder. What if Jesus had arrived on the earth with the equivalent of a name tag? What if there were no mistaking him for just another person? Can you imagine the stick-on label?

Hi! My name is:

Jesus, the Son of God, the Messiah

95

Now wait a minute, Dan! you protest. *Don't you Bible-totin' types always say that Jesus' arrival was heralded? With a lot of hoopla. Big-time doings. The sky gets bright. An angel appears. Gets out his bullhorn and cranks up the volume. No little announcement there!*

And aren't you always claiming that God didn't stop with that? A legion of heavenly messengers splits the night sky. The trumpets come out. The choir tunes up. Glorifying God. Whooping it up. A kind of heavenly "toast" to God for the birth of his Son.

And you haven't forgotten the shepherds, have you? The first "Hallelujah!" and they're high-tailing it to the nearest foxhole to hide in. The second "Hallelujah!" and they're ready to tell the world!

Sure enough. There was a lot of activity. Right then. But did you notice that things sort of quieted down after that? After Herod gets into a royal rage and sends his executioners to slaughter the baby boys of Bethlehem, and Mary and Joseph make an end run to Egypt, we don't hear "word one" about Jesus until he is Bar Mitzvah and knocks the socks off the Torah professors in Jerusalem. That's eleven years without hearing the name "Jesus of Nazareth."

Then there is silence once again. About seventeen years worth of silence about the Son of Man. What Jesus did as a teenager we don't know. It's a good guess that he received an education in town, then went on to learn his father's carpentry trade as an apprentice, stepping in as a full-time furniture maker when Joseph died. But it's only a guess. Scripture doesn't say. At any rate, the next time we meet Jesus is shortly after his thirtieth birthday.

If we were in charge of public relations, we would have insisted that Jesus' name get out in front of the public early — and stay there. Right from his birth to his ratification as God's only son at his dedication by John the Baptist. Can you imagine the scene at the press gathering? Those unfortunate enough to be on the outside of a mob of news correspondents strain to hear:

Yes, that's right, Jesus — J - e - s - u - s. Got that? Mother's name is Miriam. Ancestry, tribe of Judah. Line of David. True father's name is Yahweh. Earthly father/caretaker name is Joseph.

Also of David's line. Birthplace was Bethlehem, prophesied in Scripture. Fled to northern Africa during Herod's pogram against the male infants, then returned to live in Nazareth — also foretold in the Word of God. Graduate of Jerusalem University. Plans to teach and preach. Was designated by the Almighty to be Israel's Messiah and Savior of the world, Jews and Gentiles included. A complete press release kit will be available at 2:00 this afternoon. Jesus isn't offering a statement right now, but will have a full press conference next Wednesday at 9:00 in the morning. Thank you, ladies and gentlemen.

God chose no such hype for the introduction of Jesus. Not when he began to teach the Kingdom in parables. Not when, as an adolescent, he was part of the Jewish coming-of-age ritual. Not when he was "subject to Mary and Joseph" as a child learning discipline. And not when he was born.

The fact is that, except for a few well-chosen moments, the entirety of Jesus' human sojourn was marked by its customary, commonplace, and ordinary character. This was an intentional and deliberate act, well thought out by God. Here are the reasons why he carried out his intent in just this way.

First, it was not God's plan to intimidate us into subjection. God could have put on an awesome display of raw power. God could have had humanity so thoroughly terrorized that they would have gladly embraced him out of fear. But the Bible makes it clear that, from the first, God's desire was to enjoy a relationship of loving friendship with the creatures of his making. If you didn't know it, that's what God's Word is putting forth in the story of creation: "Let us make humankind in our image, according to our likeness" (Genesis 1:26).

God wanted to commune with us. God wanted to speak with us. God wanted to laugh with us. God wanted to be with us. And Jesus presented his divine nature through — what? Through friendship with those he taught. That is why the Twelve followed him. That is why the crowds "listened to him eagerly." That is why children ran toward, not away from, his outstretched arms. That is why cynics, whose hearts were unresponsive and whose minds were closed, still found an inexaustible reservoir of patience and understanding. Shepherds and kings alike were shown the same warmth, welcome, and wonder.

Second, the Incarnation was not intended as a condemnation but as a proclamation. "[S]ee — I am bringing you good news of great joy for all the people: to you is born this day in the city of David a Savior, who is the Messiah, the Lord" (Luke 2:10-11).

The appearance of God's messengers — human and angelic — was often seen to precede some kind of disaster. The truth is that humanity's disobedience had forged that sort of unfortunate reputation. And that's why the men in the Bethlehem fields were about to make a run for the nearest explosion-proof bunker. But God's winged witness made a quick explanation to the shivering shepherds. "Wait a minute! God has something wonderful that he wants to share with you! At long last, it is good news. God isn't going to destroy; he's going to save."

Heaven sent an angel to announce that the time of sinners' release was not merely imminent, but present. However, did you note that the only recipients of the news were a bunch of Bethlehemite shepherds who were guarding the flocks of Passover-bound creatures? In ancient Palestine, there was virtually no one on a lower social stratum than a keeper of sheep. Shepherding was regarded as the most common of all tasks. What better group to fit into God's plan of salvation! Anonymous types ... commoners ... blue-collar "working stiffs" who'd find no social compunction not to tell everybody what they had seen and experienced.

Kings? They would share the news with their fellow blue-bloods. Scholars? They'd converse only with their contemporaries in the academic world. Theologians? They would probably talk themselves out of believing that such a thing was possible. But shepherds had nothing to lose. And the world had everything to gain.

Third, Jesus was sent from the heart of God to redeem sinners, not saints. The Bible says, "For it is clear that he [Christ] did not come to help angels, but the descendants of Abraham.... Because he himself was tested by what he suffered, he is able to help those who are being tested" (Hebrews 2:16, 18).

Jesus of Nazareth looked like us, talked as we talk, worked the same as we do, suffered in the same way that we experience hurt, and shared everything that is common to our lives. Jesus was so much a part of us, in fact, that the prophet Isaiah wrote this in anticipation of his advent: "[H]e had no form or majesty that we should look at him, nothing in his appearance that we should desire him" (Isaiah 53:2).

If he had been a pedestrian trying to negotiate Manhattan's Seventh Avenue during the rush hour, you wouldn't have noticed. If he had been a fellow sitting on a bench in view of the Kremlin, you would not have turned aside to look. If he had been a hot, dusty traveler pausing at the side of a road leading into Addis Ababa in Ethiopia, you wouldn't know who he was or where he had come from or what he was going to do. He was just that indistinguishable from the rest of the crowd. He wasn't taller, broader, or more handsome than the average Joseph or Zachariah. Intentionally so. Jesus identified himself with us so that we could lose ourselves in him.

Incidentally, it also happens to explain what Jesus meant when he told his disciples to feed the hungry, shelter the homeless, clothe the naked, and visit the prisoner. He said, "[J]ust as you did it to one of the least of these who are members of my family, you did it to me" (Matthew 25:40).

- That man for whom you just bought a cup of coffee on a cold and blustery day ...
- That woman to whom you presented a coat because her threadbare jacket was falling apart ...
- That child on whom you just conferred a bit of wisdom ...
- That fellow-sinner in whose soul you just deposited a word from the precious gospel ...
- That convict with whom you shared of yourself by listening to his fears ...

Could it just be that person was a brother or a sister of Jesus?

Was it just your imagination, or did you catch a fleeting glimpse of the Savior's smile in his face? Did you see a glimmer of the Messiah's radiance in her eyes?

Remember: The gift of love doesn't come with a label. Neither does the person to whom you give it.

17
A Parable

Galatians 4:4-5

A certain man went to a builder of boats in order to have a boat made according to his specifications. He looked about the shop, observed the fine tools, and cast an observant eye upon several photographs of vessels which the craftsman had made. "Sir, you are known as one who does more than merely wield hammer and saw in a skillful way," said he. "You are recognized as an artist, and from what I can see, that title is well-deserved." Pointing to the photographs, he exclaimed admiringly: "Seldom have I seen such striving for perfection!"

The boatwright smiled as he finished reading the detailed plans which had been presented to him. *Here is a man who obviously loves the sea, who enjoys the art of sailing, and who knows boats,* said he to himself. *He will put the vessel I make to good use.*

Small wonder that the boatwright so reasoned. For the most exacting details of the vessel had been calculated and laid out upon the blueprint. Its length and breadth. The height of its mast. The size and placement of its keel. The curve of its lines. Down to the last millimeter and fraction of an angle, everything had been planned.

And no expense was to be spared! Only rare, hand-selected, blemish-free wood was to be used in the boat's construction. The sails were to be made of the finest, sturdiest cloth available. Every digital, state-of-the-art navigational aid and communication device was to be installed. Fittings would be solid brass, not brass-plated steel. The latest high-tech polymeric finishes were to coat the deck and hull with a rock-hard, weather resistant protection.

Knowing full well that such a project would be costly, the man placed a sizable sum of money into the boatwright's hand. "I will not place you under the constraint of time," he said. "Take as long as you need to finish the project. This money is to be used for materials, for implements, for your time, labor, and skill."

"And please do not hesitate to contact me to secure more funds," he urged the boat maker, "for I realize that what I have asked you to build is very costly. But I am both willing and able to pay for all of it."

Then the builder of boats gave this assurance to his new client: "I will be glad to create the sort of exquisite craft that you have so carefully thought out. I promise that you will be delighted with it."

Immediately the work began. Or rather it should be noted that first, a considerable amount of advance work had to be accomplished.

What preparation! Every piece of wood lying about the shop, depending on its size and condition, was either moved to a storage shed or thrown into a trash barrel, as were partially-used cans of paint, varnish, and thinner. In order to make the work area dust-free, the boatwright first swept, then painted, the entire floor.

He installed more lighting fixtures; the artisan wanted to make certain he could see clearly that each of the boat's flat surfaces was truly flat and level, that each of its curved surfaces was smooth and free of variation, and that the mast was perfectly plumb. Finally, he replaced a number of worn-out tools and purchased special new ones.

In short, he wished to create a vessel which was both worthy of the sea and worthy of his reputation as master craftsman.

Months passed. The work progressed. It would not be a trite thing to say that the time, effort, and care which the boatwright put into his work were aptly described as a labor of love. For he brought more than his muscles and his brain to bear on the project; he applied his very heart and soul.

And then, late one night, when every last detail was finished ... when the time was right ... when the last coat of varnish had dried ... when the last stitch had been taken in the sail ... when the last check of the radio and radar had been made ... when the last doubt that the vessel was less than perfect had been removed from his mind ... it was only then that the builder of boats, the creator of excellent sailing vessels, allowed himself to breathe a sigh of satisfaction, laid down his tools, stepped back from his work — and smiled.

Early the next day, he informed his client that the boat was ready. "The boat is yours, sir," he said when the man arrived. Then, with justifiable pride, he added, "It is ready to sail this very moment, if you so choose. It will take you wherever you wish to go on the open sea. It is absolutely watertight, so have no fear to ride it upon calm waters or rough. Storms may batter against it, but steer for deep water, and it will not fail you. My friend, use it well and often, for it is a wonderful craft."

As the craftsman came to the end of his speaking, a thin smile crept over the new boat owner's face, and he slowly shook his head from side to side. "No, no," he said evenly. "I do not intend to sail this boat. It is far too precious for that! Who is to say that an unexpected gale from the sea may take this beautiful creation and toss it upon rocky shoals?

"Or perhaps in the friendly environment of clear and warm waters, barnacles may attach themself to the pristine finish that now glistens like diamonds in the sunlight.

"Or how terrible it would be that my walking upon the deck of this exquisite vessel should scuff its surface!

"Far better," he continued, as he held up a silencing hand to the now-protesting boatwright, "far better that it receive the best possible treatment, away from the ravages of sand and surf, in a magnificent display which I have installed in my home. There it will be safe. There it will be cool and dry. There it will remain, as perfect and precious as it is at this moment."

And then the maker of beautiful boats was sad. Because he knew the purpose of boat-building is not to create a museum piece but to create a useful vessel. It exists to ply the sea, to slice through the waves of the deep, to carry its owner to new vistas and possibilities.

Long ago, a loud cry went up from the earth to the heavens. The people had sinned. They were estranged from God. They missed God's love. They lamented their outcast state. They felt themselves lost — and indeed they were lost. They were floating in a sea of sin, struggling to keep above the water, clutching onto scraps of good works as life preservers — but even they were crumbling.

Their call for help did not go unanswered. God listened to their cries. In fact, had you been with God in eternity, before time started to be reckoned and before sin entered the world, you would have seen God working on the problem. You would have seen God's love for humanity causing him to bring forth the most breathtaking plan that the world would ever see.

You can almost see a cluster of angels nearby, looking intently at the Almighty as he sits enthroned, trying to see into that great impenetrable Mind.

Presently, a smile comes across God's face as he determines what he will — no, what he must — do. Aware of the angels' presence (aware, too, of their obvious curiosity), God turns toward them. "Please," he says, beckoning them to come to him, "I want to tell you what I am going to do."

He tells them of the way by which the people can be saved from destruction. He says it will be a short route for some, a long and arduous journey for others, and an impossible road for many, since the way is gained by faith, and not all will be willing to travel that way. "I will send judges to point the way," he says. "I will send kings who will lead and point the way. I will send good men and women who will speak in my name and point the way. I will send prophets who will demonstrate my truth in their lives, and point the way."

But what God says next makes the angels gasp, both in wonder and in consternation. "Understand, though, that neither judge nor king, neither prophet nor righteous man or woman, is the way. I do not intend to send another to be the way. For I — I myself — will be the way. And I will go to them.

"I will be their King and their Servant, Teacher and Listener, Master and Friend, Shepherd and Lamb."

"How can this be?" say the angels to their Creator. "I already have a plan," he answers. "Since the people cannot become one of us, I will become one of them." At this, God bids his messengers hold their peace, for they have begun to object. "There is no other way," he reminds them. They agree. It has to be done. And so it is.

Perhaps you know the rest of the story.

The heavenly Father made sure that the most exacting details of his advent on the earth would be calculated and laid out upon the blueprint of his Word: how he would become man ... how he would appear in King David's royal line ... how he would be born of a Jewish virgin ... how he — Jesus of Nazareth — would rise in obscurity and live in poverty.

The Creator made certain that sinners would know of his plan for their salvation: through his breaking bread with them ... through his friendship and laughter among them ... through his teaching them ... through his healing them ... through his great, loving passion for them ... through his taking their sin upon himself ... through his dying in their place ... through his rising again ... through his justifying their every hope in him.

Everything had been thought out. Nothing was left to chance. Oh, what preparation! Months turned into years, and years into centuries. And the work progressed.

It would not be a trite thing to say that the time, effort, and care which the Creator put into his plan were aptly described as a labor of love. For he brought more than his muscles and his brain to bear on the project; he applied his very heart and soul.

And then, "late in time," when every last detail was finished ... when the last stitch had been taken in the fabric of the Father's masterpiece ... when the last second had ticked off the clock ... it was only then that he, the Builder of impossible dreams, the Creator of humanity's hope, and the Author of grace, allowed himself to breathe of sigh of satisfaction, laid down his tools, stepped back from his work — and smiled.

Down to the last piece of the historical and spiritual framework, all things came together at the right time. As Paul would later declare in amazement: "When the fulness of time had come, God sent his Son, born of a woman, born under the law, in order to redeem those who were under the law, so that we might receive adoption as children" (Galatians 4:4-5).

It was God's crowning achievement. Nothing compared to it. The creation of the heavens and the earth was certainly more grandiose. The liberation of the sons of Israel from enslavement was more epic. And the development of a chosen nation was unprecedented.

But the incarnation of God in Jesus Christ would stand apart. By it would be announced the only worthy vessel by which the imperfect could navigate the treacherous sea to the perfect. It would be God's new promise. God's free gift. God's final answer.

And then, in the dead of night on a Judean hillside dotted with with sleepy sheep and watchful shepherds, heaven made the announcement that the moment of God's arrival had come. With the brilliance of joy and the unmistakable message that victory now belonged to those who had been powerless to help themselves, the angel spoke: "[T]o you is born this day in the city of David a Savior, who is the Messiah, the Lord" (Luke 2:11).

God said, "The work is done, my dear children." Then, with justifiable pride, he added, "The gift of my Son ... my very self in the flesh ... the redemption of your souls ... the nourishment of your eternal spirit ... is ready for you to take.

"He will grow in knowledge and in strength. He will surpass the prophets and elders in wisdom. He will heal your broken-heartedness. He will walk with you in cameraderie and fellowship. He will dry your tears and understand your misgivings.

"He will not reject you when you doubt. He will lift the burden of your sin from your shoulders. He will go to death rather than see you perish. He will rise from the grave rather than see you despair.

"My friends, use this gift well. Put your trust in this living and dynamic Son of mine, for he will never fail you."

But alas, with the passing of years, God's message was met, not with acceptance, but with resistance. "No, no!" the people said. "We do not intend that this beautiful gift of the Christ child be disturbed. Shall the Babe of Bethlehem grow? He is far too precious for that! Look at the infant King, asleep on the hay."

"My children," cried God, "do not do this! The Child must grow. And yes, the Child will grow, in spite of you. For was it not prophesied that Christ must be born, and minister to the needs of the world, and suffer for righteousness' sake, and die to take sinners' iniquity away? Toward this end did I plan. For this purpose was he born."

But the people were steadfastly obstinate. "There in the cattle stall is he sung sweet lullabies by Mary his mother," they insisted. "There does he bask in the light of his natal star. There is he protected by the angelic legions of heaven. There is he under the watchful eye of Joseph. There is he adored by awe-struck shepherd bands.

"There, curled up in his nest, he is far from Herod's wrath ... from lonely days ... from dusty roads ... from the pain of humanity ... from bitter rejection ... from misunderstandings ... from stinging betrayal and unjust accusation ... from Pilate's house ... from Calvary.

"And there," they said, with a sweep of the hand toward the place where the baby Jesus was lying, "there shall he stay."

The heart of the Creator was saddened. Because of their great and terrible loss. For he knew what would happen. And so it was —

- They sang the songs of the Savior's birth, but not the songs of his grace.
- They remembered a star's light over Bethlehem, but not God's light over them.
- They bore witness to the sweetness of Jesus' countenance, but not to the strength of his will.
- They believed in the Christ-child's power to charm, but not in his power to forgive, restore, and lift the sinner to heaven.

So annually, they made merry for a season. But something was missing from their celebrations.

- They spoke of love come down at Christmas, yet walked alone.
- They spoke of joy to the world, yet wondered why it was not theirs.
- They spoke of peace among men, yet had none in their hearts.

For years, they worshiped before a tableau which to them had become a symbol, not of the strong, eternal Savior, but of a sort of generalized and nebulous warmth which they experienced on their annual journey through Christmastime.

And then, on one terrible day, they could remember no longer why they visited it at all.

107

18
Why Is This Night Different?

Exodus 12:26

It is 9:30. It is nighttime, Christmas Eve. There is a cold wind blowing in from the northwest, moisture is pushing in from the south, and the barometer is sinking like a stone, a sure sign of snow. Overhead, the cloudy sky is low, leaden, and bright with reflected light from city streets.

I turn my collar up against the chill. Lynne pulls her scarf over her mouth and nose. The children yank their coat zippers as high as they will go. Almost as if we are taking directions from an unseen conductor, we start singing "Joy To The World" in six-part harmony. Mostly because of happiness. Partly because it gets our adrenaline flowing. We crunch through the snow.

The first service of Christmas Eve is history. The Christ candle on the Advent wreath has been lit, the musicians have played, the choir has sung, the congregation has caroled, and I have preached. Now, the church is temporarily empty.

The sexton has kept the church's electric candelabra on. A minute ago, we exited the church in their warm glow. When we got to the sidewalk, Lynne looked back at them and remarked how beautiful they were.

We approach the house. We see a pair of noses push aside the curtains. This is followed immediately by a duet of muted woofs and howls. As we open the front door, we are greeted by a breath of warm air ... and two beagles.

It is Christmas Eve, and it occurs to me, as it always does, that something is different. The stores are actually, finally closed. The last CD has been bought. The last sweater has been tried on. The last fast-food restaurant burger has been flame-broiled. The last credit card has been plunked down in front of a weary clerk. The last cookie has been baked. All over, doors are being locked and season's greetings are being exchanged by store managers and their employees.

But the fact that cash registers are now silent is not what I distinguish as different this night.

I note that in their home-sewn red and green dresses, my beloved Lynne and our daughters Shana and Kyrsten, are positively aglow tonight. Son Daniel — and son-in-law Chris — are handsome in their favorite navy blue suits. I pop a Christmas music cassette into the tape deck. Kyrsten sits on the living room rug and plays with the dogs. Shana puts finishing touches on a handmade gift. Daniel makes cocoa for Santa Claus. Lynne rearranges a few tree decorations. Chris whistles to the cockatiel. Not a single overhead light fixture or table lamp is on anywhere in the house, but the place is as bright as if we had every one of them turned on full power. We read, play, and bustle around the kitchen by the light of Christmas trees, candles, and kerosene lanterns that seem to make the house pulse with a multi-colored warmth.

But the fact that the television is off, that soft music, soft light, and soft conversation fill the air, and that a certain seasonal elegance is reflected by all the inhabitants of our dwelling place, are not the reasons that I know this night to be different.

It occurs to me that there was something odd about walking home from the church. It was not a sound, but the absence of familiar sounds, that called my attention to it. There were cars on the road, but tonight, their drivers were not maniacal pilots of guided missiles, jockeying for the first position in front of traffic lights and vying to see who might go the fastest from one end of town to the other. Tonight there was no foul stench of cursings and profanities which are regularly spit forth from street corners and automobiles and storefronts. In their stead, the sweet fragrance of little children's laughter and family conversation and the love songs of those who have been couples for forty and fifty years.

But the fact that for one brief moment, there is a strange and marvelous stillness in the midst of what had appeared to be a perpetually noisy world — that is not what is different about this night.

110

I have pondered this mystery many times. It is 9:30, Christmas Eve, and I contemplate it anew. Suddenly, I find myself a kindred spirit with a son reclining at the Passover table, asking the question that has been repeated by sons for thousands of years: *What is it about this night that makes it different from all others?* For him, the answer is spread out plainly, as it has been since that terrible, wonderful night that was Israel's last under the oppression of Egypt:

> *Observe the month of Abib by keeping the passover to the Lord your God, for ... the Lord your God brought you out of Egypt by night.... For seven days you shall eat unleavened bread — the bread of affliction — because you came out of the land of Egypt in great haste, so that all the days of your life you may remember the day of your departure ..." (Deuteronomy 16:1, 3).*

But as to why this night — Christmas Eve — is unlike other nights: that is what I seek to know.

I wonder. Do you? Do you ever find a fascination with the unusual happenings and curious behavior among human beings at this extraordinary time of year? Would you, as I, like to discover why a lot of people suddenly speak civilly to one another? Why we extend courtesies that we do not even think of any other time? Why claws are withdrawn and fangs are covered over in our relationships? Why in time of war, arms have been laid down and sworn enemies have embraced one another and toasts have been lifted up in each other's honor, if only for a few hours or a day? Why there is talk of love and loveliness, of hope and help, of giving and thanksgiving?

I have wondered about these things. I suspect you have, too.

For the answer, it is necessary to take a journey. A journey back through time to a world so much like our own that we have to make certain we have actually made the trip. You need to know that it is not just any time, but a singular moment in history.

- Like ours, that world is filled with anger, hatred, malice, political intrigue, and murder.
- Like ours, that world makes money its god, and makes God its enemy.

111

- Like ours, that world calls good evil, and evil good; justice is vilified and corruption is sainted.
- Like ours, that world abounds with loneliness, frustrations, and heartache.
- Like ours, it too is a world of great sadness.
- Like ours, it too is a world of an overwhelming sense of hopelessness.

Yet in an almost-forgotten corner of that world, in an instant of time, something momentous has just happened. It will have a profound effect on every moment to come, on every facet of history from then on.

That "something" is not properly called an "event," in the usual sense of the word. An event arrives heralded and published and greeted with great throngs of people. But at this milestone there are no reporters, no spotlights, and no engraved invitations. It is easy to overlook, to walk by, or to ignore.

But that this great occurrence in the history of humankind comes unannounced or with great fanfare does not make the night different.

That which has just happened is not discussed in the great halls of government. Nor is it analyzed in centers of economy. Nor do captains of industry even note it. In fact, the powerful, the rich and the influential are not present at all. The commoner is. The poor man is. The blue-collar worker is. The unsophisticated person is. Still, the night is not different because of them, plain or fancy.

In fact, observing it as a disinterested spectator, I mark this incident as a total non-event which affects me not in the slightest — only the actors who are immediately present: a hungry infant, just delivered; his exhausted but happy mother; his beaming father; and a few curious bystanders who try to peek at the newborn's face. The birthing couple is homeless ... not unusual, then or now. The world doesn't hold its peace until the baby goes to sleep ... not unusual, then or now. The press and the noise of commerce, carousal, and consternation goes on unabated ... not unusual, then or now.

But viewed through the lenses of faith, this scene takes on an aspect of uniqueness that is unrivaled in any age. For here and now

I know that God has again staked his claim upon a world whose inhabitants had long been gripped by terrible fears. Fear of their own failure. Fear of the future. Fear of death. Fear of judgment. Fear of the awful darkness beyond.

And then I realize: it is not the world that has changed this night! Tonight, the stars are still fixed in their courses. Tonight, the clouds will still drop snow, or rain, or nothing at all.

Tonight, the blare of business will continue without pause. Tonight, the shrill cacophony of profanity and blasphemy will continue to pour forth on street and sidewalk. It is I who have undergone change!

Here in Bethlehem ... here in a hillside cave that passes as a crude stable ... here beside a horse-and-mule feeding-trough ... here next to a frightened, exhilarated teenaged mother and her confused, awestruck husband do I know that God has pitched his tent and taken up residence — by me!

Here and now do I know why most will pass by and never see what has happened: "He was in the world, and the world came into being through him; yet the world did not know him. He came to what was his own, and his own people did not accept him" (John 1:10-11).

Here and now do I know why the gift of Christmas was so costly to God: "For God so loved the world that he gave ..." (not loaned, not sold, but gave) "... his only Son, so that everyone who believes in him may not perish but may have eternal life" (John 3:16).

Here and now do I know why the music and the pageantry and the splendor of Christmas drown out the sounds of rancor and rage: "But to all who received him, who believed in his name, he gave power to become children of God ... From his fulness we have all received, grace upon grace" (John 1:12, 16).

Here and now do I know why his name had to be Jesus, for his name in Hebrew (the name given him before his birth by the angel of God) — the name Yeshua — tells me why he was born: "... for he will save his people from their sins" (Matthew 1:21).

Here and now do I know why it no longer matters what happens in the world tonight — for the nations will still rage and truth will still be the beggar crying out to be heard and justice will be scorned and God will still be cursed — because I am told by the Man who grew up from the baby: "But take courage; I have conquered the world!" (John 16:33).

It is 9:30. It is nighttime, Christmas Eve. There is a cold wind blowing in from the northwest, moisture is pushing in from the south, and the barometer is sinking like a stone, a sure sign of snow. Overhead, the cloudy sky is low, leaden, and bright with reflected light from city streets.

And I finally know what makes this night unlike any other night in the history of creation: I am no longer alone.

19
First Sunday Of Advent

Meditation

Come, thou God of earth and heaven;
Now thine own, thy people, save!
Lest by sin's gross degradation,
We — in error — darkness crave.

Prayer

Blessed God, we thank you that, in the quietness of thought and in the secret place of the spirit, you remind us of your greatness. In this season particularly, keep our minds focused upon the wonder of your redeeming love.

We ask this through the merit of Jesus Christ, who is King of kings, and reigns over all creation.

Amen.

20
Second Sunday Of Advent

Meditation

Justice, peace and hope are driven
From the earth by base design.
Judge of all the meek and faithful:
To us bring some sacred sign.

Prayer

O God, at this season of the advent of your only begotten Son, may our morning prayers cease to be our boring prayers.

Let our spirits be as alive, alert, awake, and attuned to the harmonies of heaven as we rise to greet you at the beginning of the new day, as our ears thrill to the music of earth which sets the blood coursing through our bodies.

Lord God, may the generations-old song "Joy to the world! The Savior reigns!" be the new song of your church, your congregation, and yes, our very being.

Thank you, blest Creator and Redeemer, for the prophets' hope, for Joseph's faith, for Mary's willingness, for the angels' joy, and for the shepherds' response. May the rhythm of their song be the start of a new song — an eternal song — in our lives.

This we ask in Jesus' precious and strong name.

Amen.

21
Third Sunday Of Advent

Meditation

Strong name of gracious love,
Be with us 'til the morrow!
O God, be ours always,
To drive out fear and sorrow!

Prayer

You have given without measure, O God! You have sent your only-begotten Son — the pure and undefiled Image of your Being, the Light of life, and the Joy of heaven — to take our nature upon himself. How can this be, gracious Lord? Yes, and how can we say our thanks for the gift that goes beyond measure?

Grant that what we do in this season may be true worship, honest prayer, and Godly praise. May we always remember that we honor you with our lives, where mere words utterly fail.

Renew us this day, as in all days, by your Holy Spirit.

This we ask through Christ our Lord.

Amen.

22
Fourth Sunday Of Advent

Meditation

Lord of Hosts, we need thy presence:
Dark and doubt obscure our way;
Sin abounds; temptations draw us.
Turn, and come to us today!

Prayer

Fill us, O God, with such wonder, gratitude, and love, that with shepherds, and kings, and countless hosts of pilgrims the world over, we may always approach the birth of the holy Child with reverence, adoration, conviction, and utter consecration.

As you came in the stillness of night, Almighty Father, enter our lives by faith in the quietness of this sacred moment. Overcome our spiritual darkness with the great and eternal light of Christ's presence, so that we may clearly see that he is the way to walk, he is the truth to speak, he is the life to lead all the days of our life and forever.

Let our worship of him be pure, strong, confident, and unafraid that we may sing your praises before the world.

Blessed God, this is the prayer that we raise to you in the strong name of Christ Jesus, our Savior and Lord.

Amen.

23
Christmas Eve

Meditation

Everyone, come greet the day
Of mirth and cheer! With angels say,
"Christ is born! Salvation's here!
In humble birth, our God's drawn near."
Gloria! To Him be praise;
To Jesus e'er ring out the bells.
Earth holds not a greater joy
Than God-with-us, Emmanuel!

Prayer

O Christ Jesus, Prince of peace and Lord of heaven and earth: Multiply our joy this night! Grant us the wonder of a little child whose wide-eyed delight at Christmas reaches forth to receive a gift without pause, question, or suspicion. Let us, too, with no hesitation, stretch forth again our willing spirits, with eager anticipation and heart-pounding expectation, to claim that marvelous, miraculous gift of your self, which was bestowed in unselfish, sacrificial and joyful love.

This we ask in your strong name.

Amen.

24
Christmas Day

Meditation

Now lift up voices, sing his praise
Whose birth all heaven and earth unites
In joyous wonder, love and mirth:
Christ the Lord, God's true-born Light.

Prayer

Awaken our enthusiasm for Christ, O God in heaven, as cold winter air brings a flush to the cheeks and a pulse to the heart. May we
no longer be content with simply spending one pleasant hour with
him on Christmas Day in the atmosphere of pew and pulpit. By the
Holy Spirit, may we be enabled to dedicate every moment to honor
and serve him who is King of kings and Lord of lords, whether in
the workplace or in the marketplace, whether home or away,
whether in season or out of season.

Thus renewed in the inner man or woman, may we be put to
work in the harvest field, in which the bounty is the turning of lost
souls to the Lord Jesus. We pray that you would add to our joy, our
determination, and our excitement.

We ask it in the name, and for the sake, of Jesus Christ, our
Savior and Lord.

Amen.

www.ingramcontent.com/pod-product-compliance
Lightning Source LLC
LaVergne TN
LVHW021521080426
835509LV00018B/2597